Louis Reed

I AM A WILD REBELLE WITH A CAUSE!
MY MODUS OPERANDI IS: CELEBRATING THE SACRED ART ALCEHMY.

As a Visionary Artist, Author and Teacher my commitment to stopping violence against women inspires me to use creativity as a medium to deepen our connection to the Divine Feminine within and to raise awareness of the importance of gender equality creating a more integrated world were the best of the masculine and feminine work in harmony.

I am passionate about working with women to journey within to connect to their heart and soul so their wild creative spirit can be awakened. I believe wholeheartedly that creativity heals and transforms at a deep, soul level. Not just healing us but also healing the collective consciousness of mother earth.

My artworks have been sold and sent worldwide. I teach locally, nationally and internationally, inspiring women to connect to their Divine Feminine though the lens of the Wild Woman Archetype and to awaken their creative self.

Join our Wild Rebellion today!

THE LEGEND OF THE RED THREAD SAYS:

```
"Those who are suppose to meet
are connected by an invisible red thread
        since before birth.
      It can stretch and tangle
      But it will never break."
```

I invite you to enter the quantum field of connection through imagination. Using your imagination guides you towards seeing how you are part of the weave of connection, contributing to it and are essential to how it works. There are many layers to connection – let's begin with three. You and your peers, you and those you are calling, and you within the greater weave of humanity.

To know what is your to cause and create is to choose to be a part of the revolution of awakened ones. Awakened ones are self-expressed beings.

I invite you to mend the world and yourself with Red Thread woven from the heart of the world soul.

RED THREAD CAFÉ

Is a sacred space in which lives are changed? It is a daily ritual designed to enable you to show up in your life and do your sacred work in the world – to hand you the thread of empowerment. This is the way that will lead you towards not only what YOU need, but also what the world needs from you.

Through the Read Thread Café you are empowered to:
- Show up and do your service in the world
- Discover and share your gifts
- Learn what you care about and express it in community
- Call your tribe together around what matters to all of you
- Discover and deepen your content
- Guide others to share their gifts and deepen their content
- Practice the power of intention to open hearts and minds
- Create a space for shared wisdom and education

THE WAY OF THE RED THREAD

CONNECTION
We are already and always connected.
Our lives have led us to this moment to recognition.
Our connection helps us to trust that we are part of a story
Greater than our own, that we are not alone.

RESPONSIBILITY
We are each only responsible for holding our
own piece of the red thread.
We hold a piece of the greater thread that is an essential
part of the fabric of the world.
Our potential to hold ow own piece is not destiny but a
potential which we can make ourselves available to
With our yes, or not.

INTENTIONALITY
We engage with a specific intention
to increase our capacity.
We apply intention and attention into
the rituals of the Red Thread.
Intentional focus amplifies energetic and
Physical shifts for ourselves and those we sit in circle with.
We are creating a field of possibility.

TRANSFORMATION
We weave our threads together and transform.
Witnessing one another's stories changes the stories that run our lives.
The capacity for breaking through from sharing ourselves and stories
enables the possibility to heal and bless ourselves, others and the world.

THE WISDOM BLESSING

May you choose outrageous actions
that challenge who you are
And encourage who you are becoming.

May you take one step, however small,
towards that which you have already longed for.
Now is the right time!

May you recognise the unique
and powerful contribution that you bring
to the people whose lives you touch.

May you be as grand and wonderful as you
really are?
And do things because you want to,
not just because you should.

May you celebrate your creativity
And believe that you are and artist
With a unique vision that no one else has.

May you find peace and purpose
and passion amidst the chaos and suffering.
While remaining aware of the unrest in the world.

May you reach towards the spirit
with a longing that keeps you awake
to the miracles available all around you.

May your faith move any mountains
Standing in you way and bring you
Great teachers to awaken your understanding.

May you give up shame, guilt and self-neglect
And replace them with freedom, integrity,
And a path of self-nurturing.

May you offer the gifts and blessings of your soul
To beings of the world
When the time is right for you to release them.

May you passionately and deeply love
And be loved by someone
Who can see who you really are.

May your body speak to you
And teach you how to care
For the temple housing your bright light.

May you walk gently on the earth
And honor your hearth and family
With your action and your rest.

May you find and enjoy the fruit of abundance
so that your life path
Can be fortified and furthered.

May you embrace the Tree of Life
And be informed by the wisdom
She brings to those on Her path.

May LOVE be at the center of all you choices
And may you, with me,
Send this blessing to all beings

Aho Lou

Turn your demons into art, your shadow into a friend,

YOUR FEAR INTO FUEL,

YOUR FAILURES INTO TEACHERS,

your weaknesses into reasons to keep fighting.

Dont waste your pain. - *Andréa Balt*

CONTENTS

Welcome Wild One 11
Goddess Questionnaire 13

The Invitation 25
Heroines Journey 27
Archetypal Experiences 28

Walking the Goddess Medicine Wheel 29

Space 31
Air 37
Fire 43
Water 49
Earth 55
Alchemy 61

Aligning with the Cycles of our Life 69
An Animate World 69
Ascent & Decent Path 70
The Elements as Cycles of Creativity 70
Seasons: The Wheel of the Year 70

Moon Mysteries and Menstruation 75
Crescent Moon: Maiden Pre-Ovulation 75
Full Moon: Mother/Lover Ovulation 76
Waning Moon: Enchantress Pre-Menstruation 77
New Moon: Crone/Wise Woman Menstruation 77

Become a Force of Nature 78
Karli & Mary Magdalene 79
Triple Goddess Astrology 82
Dream Tending 85
Resources & References 88

A Note from Lou 90

WOMANIFESTO

Dream the World Awake

1. **We are editors of life.** We cut and paste its daily beauty and pain with the sharp scissors of our minds on the canvas of humanity. We tell the untold stories.

2. **We regard Art as a dynamic matter of Now.** Art is not just a museum affair. We are our own living collage of images, memories, experiences, relationships, thoughts and feelings.

3. **Life is short and it's running through our fingers.** Our hour won't come in some kind of imagined, distant or near future, our hour is happening this very moment.

4. **The only censorship we apply to ourselves is the kind that will censor other people's genuine right to be whole.** Love the way you want to be loved and recognize a piece of you in every piece of life.

5. **We avoid nothing, we want it all. Life is homemade, painful, intelligent and beautiful.** As creators, healers and Wild Women it is our duty to curate reality and communicate it in our own, unique words.

6. **We long and steer toward the light but we don't hide or get rid of the darkness.** It's only by accepting, integrating and finally reusing every bit of ourselves that we are able to meet and face life for what it is, in all its brightness and all the shadows it casts.

7. **We regard the human experience as an indivisible whole that includes all aspects of the human experience: physical, intellectual, relational, emotional and spiritual.**

8. **Hey Frodo, it's a lonely battle, and we need help taking the ring to Mordor.** In this lifehouse, we collaborate, we share and e-hug daily. We can't do this (or anything) alone. We need each other. The only way through, is together.

9. **Our shared stories create markers along a dark and weathered path.** We choose growth versus fitting in, feeling versus insensitivity, flowing water versus stagnation, and a life fully expressed versus holding our wild, writhing stories captive within.

10. **We know enough, we have enough, we are enough and we care enough to make it wonderful.** Now.

WELCOME WILD ONE

Each one of us is called to serve in some way or form. Our unfolding lives beckon us into a unique expression that, when healthy, has the whole in mind. As women we live at a powerful time in history in the Western world, where we have more choice and autonomy in our lives than ever before. Concurrently humanity as a whole continues to push forward at great peril for our earth, and perhaps, our future. During this incredible crucible it is my belief that woman hold the worldview, the innate way of being, that could move us, as Anodea Judith says, from the love of power to the power of love.

We are collectively awakening to a broader, more inclusive understanding of intelligence and leadership. Where things like intuition, compassion, empathy, sensuality, rhythm, metaphor, and our moon cycles, are realized as key competencies that need to be nurtured and brought forth. This inclusion extends to a non-hierarchical leadership model where the community, the coven, are the gurus. Where each one of us can be guide for others...into their own truth of heart - which is blessing enough, and where integral understanding, not anger or fear, dominate our worldview.

This course was born with these things in mind. As we move through this content, keep in mind we each hold sacred ceremonial space. This is space that has been held by women for thousands of years and we will treat it together with the utmost respect. The woman's way of learning is in being, not necessarily in doing; in connection, collaboration and conversation. It is non-linear, and non-hierarchical and grounded in other kinds of intelligences beyond the mental. I am not here as a leader, but as a mentor, of equal standing, my role is to simply offer from my heart my experience, strength and hope with you to help you remember your truth so that you can live the gift that is the WILD WOMAN parts of us the world so desperately needs.

Who is our Wild Woman?

As the Divine Feminine awakens on this planet, there is a great surge of all things related to the Goddess. Everywhere you can find references to Her - both in authentic, grounded and sacred ways, and in ways that are buzzy, trendy, and ego enhancing. During the course of our time together we'll seek to ground terminology in our own embodied experience, and to explain it (if it needs explaining) in ways we can all understand and apply to our evolving lives.

The Wild Woman is an archetypal quality of Self. We each have an inner wild woman inside that wants - no - needs, to be expressed and accessed. It is this very piece of ourselves that is quite dangerous for the status quo, and so has been long demeaned and held quiet. It is the one of us who is in touch with the dark swing of the wheel. The one who knows how to let things go, to follow her own council, to pull the rug back and say 'what's that?'. This is the one of us who is connected, belly to the earth, and so knows the old stories and ancient secrets in our bones.

The one that knows without fail, there is more than meets the eye. She is terrifying to anyone holding power out of integrity, and to the shaky foundation of hierarchical power structures. Because she holds herself in all of her beauty, and all of her mess, channeling the anger and grief of what as long been repressed, she is often terrifying to our own egos as well.

Becoming FERAL

Dr. Clarissa Pinkola Estes refers to the wild ones of us as FERAL. The aspects of self that have been domesticated by the over-culture: which is to say, been veiled, hidden, coerced to conform, brainwashed by the media, and squashed through misplaced power for thousands of years. But feral means what was ONCE domesticated, and has found freedom again. Living at the edge of the village - not quite of it, not quite separate from it.

We are being re-wilded through our remembering. Why? Because it is our most natural impulses that hold the power to truly change the world. And so my sisters, we are singing over the bones, stirring our ancient birthright way of being that remembers another way...one that is whole and holy, and we do it not only for ourselves, but for our people and our planet.

Safe Space

Regardless of where we are in the world, whether we are together physically in-person or spread out far and wide, we are holding sacred and safe space together. What happens in circle stays in circle. The breath that is exchanged is holy, beyond time and space, and often altered in some way - one that cannot be understood in our middle world lives. A Wild Woman knows what is to be kept secret. We have done it for thousands of years and will continue to steward the ancient magic together. Please hold all that is written here, and all that is spoken about on our journey as sacred to you. And know that the stronger the container, the stronger the magic.

Thank you for your courageous and wild heart.

GODDESS QUESTIONNAIRE

An archetype is a way of looking at over-arching types, personalities and patterns. This way of looking at our behaviors that has existed since ancient times in folklore and mythology and even prehistoric artwork; the archetype has been used in many different ways by diverse modalities.

Shedding light on our understanding of who we are, a kind of categorical exploration of humans with a kind of super-human lens. Archetypes are often used in story telling to provide a teaching, or understanding. Often, we are 'put into' archetypes based on our behaviors, what we identify with in story, or symbols that seem like to us, a stereotype.

Lets lean in and become curious about which Archetype your are embodying. Tick the boxes that applies to you.

1. ☐ I prefer being at home with family rather than going out, so clothing and make up are not all that important to me.

2. ☐ I prefer casual clothes that are comfortable rather than dressy, or stylishly tighter fitting outfits.

3. ☐ I prefer clothing that is flowing, perhaps prints, floral designs, perhaps frilly, that match the girlish part of my feelings.

4. ☐ I prefer conservatively well dressed, pant or dress suit, low-heeled shoes, minimal jewellery with my diamond wedding ring, and light make-up.

5. ☐ I love dressing up; my style is quite feminine, sexy & flatters my attractive figure. I love jewellery tastefully selected, colourful silk scarves to enhance my outfit.

6. ☐ I prefer tailored, classical clothing, some may perceive it as more masculine in style I feel more on equal footing with men dressed in this way. I'm not so interested in the latest fashion.

7. ☐ I prefer clothing that is practical rather than fashionable. I'm not interested in attracting attention to myself by my clothing; therefore, I prefer very simple styles in neutral colours.

8. ☐ I'm more connected to my thoughts & ideas than having any particular awareness of my body.

9. ☐ My body requires regular exercise physical fitness is a priority in my life. I'm o.k. With some touch I'm not interested in being fondled I prefer some emotional distance.

10. ☐ I enjoy and seek out physical touch, regularly, in my interactions with those I love. I love using scented, creamy lotions to create baby-soft skin to be touched.

11. ☐ To be honest, I don't relate much to my body it's just not in my conscious awareness as much as my awareness of my inner thoughts dreams & fantasies.

12. ☐ I'm not very interested in focusing on my body, I have more important things to tend to my activities: organizations, meetings, promoting my families' activities. I feel a bit uncomfortable dealing with concerns of the body.

13. ☐ My body is built for the nurturing of children holding, hugging. This sort of touch gives me more pleasure than any other. I'm not that concerned about sex for it's own sake unless I'm looking forward to having another child, a process that I adore.

14. ☐ I take care of my body in a manner similar to that of my home. I don't think much more of my body than it's ability to function well. I enjoy touch with my husband when it occurs; however, it's not what I'm thinking about.

15. ☐ If my home was located in a prestigious neighbourhood, the impression I seek to convey in my home: conservative elegance, I prefer a large, stately home, neat and tidy - a place to impressively entertain my partner's prominent colleagues--and where I shine as the hostess.

16. ☐ I enjoy city living - therefore, I would enjoy a condo. A 'plus' if it was near bookstores and near my work, as I tend to work long hours. You might find my laptop on my dining table along with my paper work as I'm frequently in the midst of my work.

- [ ] 17. My home often emits the smell of baking or cooking meals. I prefer a house that affords a lot of room for my family, children and children's friends to visit. My home is rarely tidy, but its well lived in and is well enjoyed by all.

- [ ] 18. I adorn my home with candles and/or other accoutrements that create a special 'mood'. I require privacy more so than a lot of visitors.

- [ ] 19. My home has strikingly tasteful colour schemes, beautiful art work, lovely art pieces, wonderful to-the-touch fabrics in my furniture, plush carpeting into which your feet sink.

- [ ] 20. I prefer country living closer to nature, than in the city. I prefer to be near a park if I live in the city so as to enjoy the trees and wildlife. In my home I prefer plants over fancy art pieces. My furniture is comfortable and simple.

- [ ] 21. My homemaker self is strong in me and loves keeping house I engage in this like a meditation. My home is neat and organized, but not rigidly so. I always have fresh cut flowers. Fresh-baked bread is something I strive for at home.

- [ ] 22. I prefer healthy organic foods to traditional store-bought foods. I eat consciously as I value a healthy, fit body. My body requires adequate protein to fuel my physical activities.

- [ ] 23. I'm more desirous of the ambiance where I dine, although I do enjoy good food - I like the sensuality of it… the experience of the textures in my mouth. I would get a kick out of feeding finger-food to my partner while sipping martinis. I enjoy the romanticness of it all.

- [ ] 24. I prefer eating out - I don't have time or interest for cooking for myself. I'd rather eat out with a friend and enjoy stimulating conversation with each other.

- [ ] 25. I love having family & children at my home to cook for. I love preparing enough food for everyone to enjoy.

- [ ] 26. Mealtimes are important family occasions although I expect people to behave with appropriate conversation and manners, as this is important to me.

- [ ] 27. Eating isn't all that important to me. I might grab a piece of cheese or whatever else my whim might be but I don't care to sit down to a meal.

- [ ] 28. Meal preparation is an important aspect of my sense of home making and I prefer to prepare nourishing meals in a quiet, unassuming manner.

- [ ] 29. Earlier, I've tended to attract partners who weren't particularly good for me creative, moody, emotional, volatile, men who fascinate me, intense relationships, partners who stir me sexually, poetically verbal individuals, unpredictability, charming, sensitive lovers. As I've matured, I prefer a sophisticated, educated partner with good taste and the means to enjoy cocktails, linen, flowers, and romance.

- [ ] 30. I've tended to be drawn to lovers who seek a maternal type of woman. I don't have high expectations of them they're more "child-like". I tend to give more than I receive. I do appreciate my partner's taking care of me, financially, as I prefer not to work outside the home. I want to feel safe and secure and focus on family and children.

- [ ] 31. I've tended to be attracted to individuals who are my intellectual equal. Their personality has a creative, artistic, healing or musical aspect. I want a partner who nurtures me. We have shared or complementary interests. We're like 'pals' enjoying activities together that we love. We give each other a lot of space that's important to me. I need them to stimulate my love of adventure. I tend to be more practical than sentimental.

- [ ] 32. I've tended to be attracted to successful partners who I tend to meet through my work life. I'm not all that flirtatious or romantic. My nature is more objective. I'm drawn to partners who are cultured and enjoy city life, intellectual and political interests. I need to be stimulated intellectually.

- [ ] 33. I've tended to attract partners to me who are my complete opposite: street-wise, tough, magnetic; sexually alluring, dominant; or those who are much older who act as my "spiritual teacher/guide" and lover. I desire a partner who understands my inner world.

- [ ] 34. I've always been attracted to upwardly mobile, powerful, successful partners who promise prominent position in the community of whom I can be proud. I've been willing to put my personal career on hold to support and to further their success.

- [ ] 35. I tend to attract partners who are drawn to my quiet, unassertive, homebody yet self-sufficient nature knowing that I will make a good wife. My partner tends to be a traditional breadwinner head-of-household type. We're both fairly independent and sex is not a priority in our relationship.

- [ ] 36. For me, sexuality and marriage are united. Initially, I tended to be more reserved, sexually. Sexuality is part of my role and what I have to offer to my partner. I've relied on my partner's expertise in arousing me, sexually. And, monogamy is essential!

- [ ] 37. When younger I was rather seductive. I am highly sexually responsive easily aroused by my lover. I prefer lovemaking as a regular part of our interactions. My attitude toward sex is more casual.

- [ ] 38. In my younger years I put my energy into my career. I tend to feel more related to my intellect than to my sexuality. I'm not so interested in sexual expression as much as other forms of expression ideas, discussions. I can be a skilful lover if I put my mind to it.

- [ ] 39. In my earlier years I was interested in having children not just having sex. I would just as soon cuddle as make love to be honest. Sexuality for it's own sake is not all that important for me making babies would satisfy me more.

- [ ] 40. Sex was like an adventure when I was younger. However, as I've matured my independence has increased; companionship, sharing activities with my partner best friend seems more important than sex.

- [ ] 41. I didn't awaken sexually until a bit later in my life. It took awhile. If the truth were told, I felt more girl-like than woman however, I felt really good about my self when I discovered my passionate, orgasmic nature.

- [ ] 42. Sex in and of itself isn't that important to me. In fact, my sexuality frequently lies dormant in me until lovemaking is initiated. I do enjoy lovemaking when it occurs it's a warm experience my partner and I share; however, I'm also fine in its absence.

- [ ] 43. I love reading, writing, keeping a dream diary, imagining, reflecting, fantasizing, I love my garden and growing plants & flowers. Although I enjoy my friends, I need plenty of alone time to renew myself.

- [ ] 44. I love collecting fine art paintings, ceramics, beautiful clothing and matching accessories/jewellery; I love attending art galleries and parties/open houses of artists. I so enjoy theatre, dance and musical performances. I delight in social occasions.

- [ ] 45. I am an avid hiker, I enjoy camping in pristine natural settings; I've enjoyed competitive sports and/or working out on a regular basis as I am naturally athletic.

- [ ] 46. I am very involved in local volunteer efforts in the community and/or in conjunction with my children's school. I receive particular pleasure being in charge and organizing. My work is something I do outside the home; however, my primary commitment is to my partner. I gear my activities and hours to match my partner's time at home.

- [ ] 47. I am very interested in reading up on the current political situations locally, nationally & abroad. I find these discussions with well-informed individuals very stimulating. I support minority group issues; I enjoy museums, lecture series, I look forward to thoughtful discussions following viewing of provocative films.

- [ ] 48. Involvement with family and close friends is my most favoured, shared activity. I love cooking for family, friends and their children as well. I find this experience so satisfying bringing everyone together sharing in a meal--the children playing together. I also enjoy sewing projects, knitting, baking, and making cookies with my children and their friends.

[ ] 49. I enjoy quiet time believe it or not, I enjoy my housework it's like a meditation for me. I focus on one chore at a time, getting into the rhythm of it without worrying about 'time'. I also enjoy reading, baking, meditation, flower arranging. On occasion I enjoy tea and sharing quiet communion with a dear friend. Occasionally I look forward to attending retreats of silence.

[ ] 50. You can usually find me in the midst of a group of men, frequently one of the only women like one of the boys in a heated political or intellectual debate. I'm not interested in the flirtatious elements in which other women engage.

[ ] 51. I feel rather shy in social situations. I'm more likely to be talking one-on-one with someone who is in need of an ear, listening to her or his concerns

[ ] 52. I would prefer being a hostess at my own social event with my husband's colleagues & their wives I like organizing and being in charge of my own event.... and to pull it off smashingly!

[ ] 53. I adore parties and social occasions I shine! I love to mingle, and flirt, and weave my way throughout the room. I definitely notice the most attractive individuals and they notice me.

[ ] 54. I'm not so keen on social events with other adults outside the venue of my friends and family. I often feel reluctant to go. I don't know what there is to talk about with these people.

[ ] 55. I tend to feel restless at social events all the flitting & flirting about that goes on. I'd rather get together with a group of my women-friends and talk about things that really matter.

[ ] 56. I don't care much for social occasions. I prefer to stay home and read a good book and enjoy my comfortable surroundings my fireplace (or if I had one).

[ ] 57. My friendships are, to a large extent, related to children my children's friends' mothers and mothers of other children. We have love of children in common as well as related family interests.

[ ] 58. I tend toward sisterly relationships/friendships with women. These relationships are very important to me I am not like other women who prefer the company of men. I am drawn to women with more feminist leanings.

[ ] 59. I'm drawn to more intellectually oriented energy in friendships. We are typically discussing work, politics, and other intellectual debates. My friends possess, as I do, strong views, articulate them well and may at times tend toward intellectual competitiveness in a sporting manner.

[ ] 60. My friends tend to be different from me I am able to be rather chameleon like. My female friends tend to have somewhat stronger personalities than I do. I have some difficulty saying 'no' at times. I tend to have difficulty putting my feelings into words. As much as I enjoy my friends, I enjoy my time to myself quite a bit.

[ ] 61. I have numerous female acquaintances. However, if my partner's job causes us to relocate, as my family is primary, I am able to pick up and move for the sake of my partner's career. This is more essential to me than friendships.

SCORE

Aphrodite
5, 10, 19, 23, 29, 37, 44, 53

Hera
4, 12, 15, 26, 34, 36, 46, 52, 61

Artemis
2, 9, 20, 22, 31, 40, 45, 55, 58

Hestia
7, 14, 21, 28, 35, 42, 49, 56

Athena
6, 8, 16, 24, 32, 38, 47, 50, 59

Persephone
3, 11, 18, 27, 33, 41, 43, 51, 60

Demeter
1, 13, 17, 25, 30, 39, 48, 54, 57

WHICH ARCHETYPE ARE YOU EMBODYING?

Athena

Athena is extroverted and independent she represents the goddess of wisdom and civilization, she is career focused and motivated by the desire to achieve, and acquire knowledge, she possesses a keen intellect, around education, culture, social issues and politics. Athena is father's daughter. She enters the male arena in the outer world. Athena is also known as one of the three Amazon women. (The myth of the Amazon women spoke of a society of fierce warrior women who lived entirely without men.) The story of her birth: she emerged, fully-grown, out of the Head of Zeus.

She is an androgynous 'virgin' goddess who develops a relationship with her own inner masculine part rather than through marriage to an outer male. Her awareness is focused. She relates to men as intellectual companion with whom she shares ambitions, career goals, and ideals. If a primarily Athenian type woman chooses partnership, she will seek one who possesses sufficient self-confidence and who will appreciate her ambition and autonomy.

A deeper look: Athena represents the feminine archetype for logical thinking as a woman, not as a man. Her virgin goddess energy can be deeply transformed or directed in highly creative ways.

By nature the virgin goddesses are more self-directed, self-motivated, focused rather than diffuse in their thinking. She is goal oriented. As a result, virgin goddess types tend toward independence and autonomy more so than their partnership-oriented vulnerable goddess sisters.

Athena's dark side: Medusa she is intimidating, critical, judgmental toward weakness in others, her air of authority and inapproachability keep others at an emotional distance.

Athena's wound: Is her heart, she is out of touch with the two goddesses of love: Demeter, the maternal love, and Aphrodite, sensual love. Her masculine image concealing her vulnerable, underdeveloped inner feminine self and she is emotionally hypersensitive.

Athena's gift: Today, is to empower women's contribute to the political, Intellectual and creative life of our cities, therefore, elevating the integrity and quality of our civilization by bringing forth the qualities of the feminine which have long been suppressed.

Historic females embodying the Athena archetype: Joan of Arc, early 1400 C.E. (a French heroine who defeated the English in battle--later burned at the stake, accused of being a witch); Christine de Pizan, 1400's C.E. (first woman in France to support herself as a writer); Mary Wollstonecraft (wrote the first great feminist document in 1792 C.E.)

Artemis

Artemis possesses an introverted and independent temperament (polar opposite to Athena) represents the goddess of Nature concerned with matters of the outdoors, animals, environmental protection, women's communities she is practical, adventurous, athletic and preferring solitude. She symbolizes regenerative earth power over all living things. Both Artemis and Athena bore arms as protectress goddesses. Historically, Artemis was born quickly by her mother, Leto. However, due to a curse from Hera, Artemis was the one who, immediately following her own birth, assisted her mother's delivery of her brother in a long and difficult labour. She became known as the patroness of childbirth.

Artemis, armed with bow and arrow, possesses the power to inflict plagues and death or to heal. She is known as the protectress of little children, baby animals and, yet, she also loves the hunt.

A deeper look: Artemis represents the feminine archetype of Nature & the Wilds virgin, pure, primitive of wild places Mother of Creatures. The function of virgins was to dispense the Mother's grace to heal, to prophesy, to perform sacred dances, to wail for the dead. Artemis' image at Ephesus depicts a torso covered with breasts conveying her as the fertile nurturer of all living things. She was also the Huntress, killer/destroyer of the very creatures she brought forth demonstrating the light and dark side of the goddess.

Artemis' dark side: Primitive power of her bloodlust, 'righteous rage' Artemis woman's task is to confront her 'inner wild boar' while sacrificing her 'righteous and avenging' goddess. She does this by humbly accepting her own flaws and mistakes as a human woman, compassionate with herself, first, then she may hold compassion towards others.

Artemis' wound: Self-esteem issues involving intimate relationship resulting from early isolation from other girls and, later, sense of rejection/exclusion by boys.

Artemis' gifts: Ability to focus, set goals and reach them; autonomy/independence, ability to develop meaningful connection with other women.

Historic females embodying the Artemis archetype:

Hildegard of Bingen a healer, poet, musician and visionary (1100's C.E.), Juliana of Norwich writer who penned "God is our Mother" in an attempt to refocus Christian awareness of her day back toward the valuation of Mother earth and the body (1300's C.E.). Modern day Artemis types: Jane Goodall, animal researcher/scientist studying chimpanzees in Tanzania for over 30 years. She also combines international animal advocacy and environment; Georgia O'Keefe-- modern artist embracing nature and combining feminine sexuality in her artwork; Peggy Callahan, wolf biologist wildlife conservation & management; Mary Jo Casalena, wild turkey biologist, studying and managing migrating birds. Billie Jean King, retired U.S. tennis pro of the late '60's and '70's.

Aphrodite

Aphrodite possesses an extroverted temperament and focuses on relationship/love she represents goddess of love (boundless eros) her primary concerns/interests are mature, adult relationships, romance, sexuality, beauty and the arts. One account of Aphrodite's birth states that she rose up from the foam on the ocean as a naked and fully developed beautiful woman; and she rode on a scallop shell.

Aphrodite represents the uniting of feminine and masculine energies through sexual union.

Aphrodite type woman admires potently masculine men and their capacity for success and combativeness. Her arena of interaction is in the boudoir or the salon. She feels comfortable with multiple relationships or extramarital affairs. She is attracted to creative men and engages with them as their inspirer. She is said to be attracted to the Son/Lover, as her romantic interests were a generation younger than she those of the sons of her godly peers.

A deeper look: Aphrodite represents the feminine archetype of relationship and love. She is adored for her beauty, her gentle manner and her amorous adventures. She has been experienced by men as fascinatingly exotic, a seductress. Her influence is of civilizing 'man' kind through her gifts of art, culture, and in particular, her disarming manner of relating. Aphrodite's divine gift to us is Eros, her divine son, also known as Cupid (Amor). Aphrodite's gift of loving relationship has the power to melt defences, leaving her lover disarmed and open- allowing the magic of eros to flow between them.

Aphrodite's dark side: The seductress, 'femme fatale'

Aphrodite's wound: Patriarchy, threatened by her 'power' over men, have attempted in every way to restrict, confine, label and demote her from her Queenly position. Aphrodite and Demeter were not allowed to co-mingle in the patriarchal order (in other words, whore and wife had to be kept separate). Aphrodite also experiences alienation from the other goddesses.

Media exploitation of Aphrodite's sacred image and the resulting schizophrenic urges to both deny [censorship] sensual beauty & pleasure while crudely lusting [graphically degrading pornography], alienation from the body, and a deep fear of intimacy [virtual reality sex on the internet/telephone sex]

Aphrodite's gifts: Her ability to be both sexual and a spiritual guide & confidante to her partner; ability to bring civility, refinement and Love into the world around her through her value of relationship and deep caring. Her compassionate nature. Her ability to inspire with eros and creativity--ecstatic, mystical gifts of love and pleasure.

Historic females embodying the Aphrodite archetype: Egyptian Cleopatra; screen actresses: Clara Bow; Greta Garbo, Marilyn Monroe, Elizabeth Taylor, Madonna

Demeter

Demeter possessing an introverted temperament (opposite to Aphrodite), a kind, gentle-soul, she re-paid people well for even the smallest favours. She is concerned with bearing, raising and nurturing children and family. Hers is a contained 'mother love'. Her awareness is diffuse.

A primarily Demeter type woman seeks a man for security rather than for intellectual or sexual companionship. In this way, the security he offers provides her a means to direct her attention to that which matters most to her home, giving birth to children and nurturing them.

A deeper look: Demeter represents the archetype of Mother. Her own grandmother was Gaia, the personification of Earth, itself. Her mother was Rhea and her father, Cronos. Archaeological evidence points to a significant Goddess cult in both the Minoan civilization of Crete (c.3000-1000 B.C.E); and the Mycenaean society of Greece (c. 1600-1400 B.C.E) suggesting her ancient matriarchal origins long before the ancient Greeks.

The expression of Demeter archetype in a woman is more than merely physical mothering; it is expressed in her instinctively obliging caring for any and all who are in need, particularly the young, needy and helpless.

Demeter's dark side: When Demeter grieved her daughter's abduction, she stopped functioning and demanded the earth stop producing-- famine threatened humankind. This destructive aspect of Demeter in Demeter type women can be seen as withdrawal--withdrawing her interests from life, from her family and friends.

Some Demeter mothers may withdraw their approval from their child when the child begins exhibiting more autonomy than Demeter woman feels comfortable with--she needs to feel needed. She may inadvertently have a need to foster dependency.

Demeter's wound: Demeter's wound is the loss, for every woman, of a particular phase of her life cycle: Maiden (innocent, untouched daughter); Mother loss of her emerging adult children into their own marriages; Crone biological loss at menopause. Each of these phases holds opportunity for emergence into a new phase of consciousness.

For Demeter type women, healing the wound may involve acknowledging 'unpleasant' feelings, feeling the 'loss' (whatever it is interpersonal or conceptual), going through the grieving process, feeling the anger and, ultimately reuniting with self on a deeper level.

Demeter's gifts: The primeval love and unity creating a magical bond between mother and daughter. Demeter nourishes spiritually as well as physically Matriarchal consciousness nurturing the earth, celebrating the cycles of life, planting, tending, giving birth and assisting in the transition called death

Historic females embodying the Demeter archetype:

Mother Teresa of Calcutta; Mary Baker Eddy, founder of the Christian Science religion; spiritual leader of Aurobindo Ashram in India known simply as 'Mother'

Hera

Hera - possesses an extroverted temperament and a focus on issue of outer world control/power. She represents goddess of marriage concerned with partnership and her relationship as wife to a man. She faces life challenges regarding power, status and leadership. Hera belongs to the relationship-oriented 'vulnerable' goddess category, suffering humiliation by her god husband Zeus. In fact, Zeus was her twin brother. He attempted, unsuccessfully, to court her so he disguised himself as a shivering little bird to obtain pity from her. His ruse worked, when she tenderly drew him to her breast, he returned to his true shape and raped her. She was shamed into marrying him. As her husband, he also shamed her by engaging in numerous extramarital sexual liaisons, further causing her humiliation. Hera had allegedly led a conspiracy against Zeus as an act of revenge.

A deeper look: Hera represents the feminine archetype of wife and matriarch of the family; she thrives in the partnership of marriage, particularly to a powerful husband whose high degree of success and prestige privileges her to enjoy position of status and power. Hera, the Greek goddess, presided over marriage and embodies the instinct to become mated.

Hera's dark side: Financial and emotional dependence on her husband her own unexplored autonomy - her unlived life apart from that of her marriage - her limited relationship to her own sexuality. Her issue - her unrecognized lust for power.

Hera's wound: Hera was denigrated by the patriarchal ancient society originally, held in esteem as a powerful and revered goddess of the sacred ritual of marriage; later demoted and disparaged as a jealous, vindictive and quarrelsome wife.

Hera's gifts: As an ancient pre-Hellenic goddess, she represents the highest form of marriage of Queen and King--of union of feminine and masculine. Hera's gift is her capacity to unite, to commit and to be a loyal and faithful partner.

Her capacity to unite, to commit and to be a loyal and faithful partner.

Hera's ideal: A complete and whole woman in her own right in honor of the feminine principle. The 'marriage' represents, psychologically, the marriage of her own feminine and masculine energies. Her partner, then, will mirror her own inner opposite qualities. She chooses, in her partner, the most longed for and most important images of her own inner, and, as yet unknown self--a major psychological undertaking and emotional work.

Historic females embodying the Hera archetype:

Queen Victoria in the 19th century and Abigail Adams (wife of President John Adams and mother of President John Quincy Adams); and Nancy Reagan.

Hestia

Hestia possesses an introverted temperament and is focused on her inner, spiritual world. Hestia is an archetype of inner centeredness. She was known to be mild mannered, upstanding, charitable, as well as a protector. She is the least known of the Olympian goddesses primarily because she never takes part in any disputes or wars. She minds her own business amidst a family of goddesses and gods who engage in 'high drama'. Similarly to Athena and Artemis she resists the amorous advances of men, therefore, placing her in the 'virgin' goddess category.

Her energy is impersonal and detached. Her awareness is focused. Different than Persephone who seeks to please others, Hestia's focus is for herself. She is grounded and her life has meaning. Unlike Athena & Artemis, Hestia did not venture out to explore the world or wilderness; she remained inside, contained within the hearth. The goddess, Hestia did not take a partner. A Hestia-type woman, today, may prefer to live a more solitary life or live within a community of like-minded, spiritual 'sisters'.

Hestia's dark side: Hestia appears to be the only goddess without an apparent dark side she avoided the drama of her 'family', refused to get 'in-the-middle' of their issues, remains calm, grounded, centred, and maintains focus on her own personal meaning

One way of thinking of Hestia's dark side if we think, metaphorically her resisting the advances made on her by both Apollo (god of Sun = intellect, logical reasoning) and Poseidon (god of Sea = the unconscious, emotion) If Hestia is seduced by these aspects: Seduced by the need for logical reasoning, she will feel compelled to dismiss her keen intuition because she is unable to 'logically explain herself'. Seduced by the unconscious, she runs the risk of becoming overwhelmed with psychic influences and/or emotional situations that keep her off balance.

Hestia's wound: In modern societies, modern woman has forfeited, for a variety of reasons, the prerogative of tending home and hearth maintaining the home fire.

Hestia's wound is more about the fact that she has little place to exist in this society with the current social values on consumerism 'having more', 'gotta have it' which requires increased work hours to enable increased spending, therefore, creating increasingly frantic lifestyle as a result.

Hestia experiences her wound when she is measured and judged by others' outer-focused, tangible standards of success, accomplishment, or marital status.

Hestia's gifts: Hestia type woman is able to enjoy her solitude not just 'here' and 'there' whenever she can 'grab a moment' but, truly enjoying her own being, consistently she is not interested in 'keeping busy' she does not enjoy 'background noise' to keep her company. Hestia offers the gift of ritual making, a powerful, affirming psychological method of honouring.

Historic females embodying the Hestia archetype:

As has been previously stated, Hestia type women do not stand out. I read about the widowed Marcella, in the 11th century C.E., who chose to live an ascetic disciplined life in her own home with her mother. She also instructed her aristocratic female friends. Domnina, 15th century C.E., lived in a hut in her mother's garden following ascetic discipline. Macrina, 10th century C.E. never married and never left her mother. She led an ascetic life at home living with her mother for some years, after which time her mother freed herself of her worldly responsibilities. Then, the two women along with their female attendants created a communal ascetic life, together

Persephone

Persephone possesses an introverted temperament (polar opposite to Hera) with issues of inner world control/power she represents the goddess of the underworld concerned with the world of spirit, the occult, matters associated with death. She is mystical, visionary and often possesses spirit guides. Her awareness is diffuse. Persephone belongs to the relationship oriented 'vulnerable' goddess category having a very close relationship with her mother, Demeter. Another aspect of her vulnerability, Persephone was abducted, taken to the Underworld and raped by Hades. Her mother, Demeter mourned, sorrowfully, in the face of her abduction.

Persephone is said to have a younger counterpart to herself Kore another name for the young Persephone. Psychologically, this may be a representation of two or three levels of this archetype. Kore, the Maiden, Persephone (or Demeter), the mature Woman, and Hecate, the Wise Crone.

Persephone type woman is more attracted to the spiritual nature rather than the physicality of her partner. She may unconsciously attract destructive relationships or potentially controlling partners. As an unconscious protective measure, she may choose a safe alternative in a younger, non-threatening partner whom she can mother.

A deeper look: Persephone represents the feminine archetype of the mediumistic mystic, connected with the spirit-world. She is also the archetypal child--radiating optimism and good hope.

Persephone's dark side - the archetypal victim - whereby she feels powerless in the midst of her circumstances - or long-sufferer/martyr - "surviving" on sympathy of others -- and, the flip side -- Hecate - the witch & killer - the one who ignored Persephone's cries -- unconscious, repressed rage which is projected onto others

Persephone's wound: A woman overly identified with the Persephone archetype will find herself repeatedly attracted to situations, people or health issues that diminish her sense of personal power. These situations/events do not appear to be her own doing they seem to happen to her, out of the blue. Yet, she seems strongly drawn to these happenings, again and again and cause her repeated grief.

Persephone's gifts: Her receptivity, intuition, empathy toward the suffering of others, her keen powers of imagination, inspiration, ability to read the hearts and minds of others. Persephone, once matured through her own inner work, is the guide to the Underworld

Historic females embodying the Persephone archetype: Florence Nightingale, Mother Teresa, Elisabeth Kubler-Ross.

FORGIVENESS
is not an occasional act,
it is a constant attitude.

THE INVITATION

What if we were able to peek between the worlds? And journey to a place where your story lives? What if we could bring healing to your story and allow you to embody your senses through accessing language and symbols you didn't even know you had access to?

What if your creative process could be a devotional act dedicated to your own healing? What if you had dire t access to your own content and information and could bring it forward? And what if this led to a deeper understanding and activation of your soul work?

Each of us is being called… Called toward a path that is uniquely ours to live and express upon the canvas of our lives. When we say 'yes' to our path, we are also saying 'yes' to move more powerfully toward that which is 'our' work to do. Our path toward our own sacred work in the world is staying true to our identity. Answering this call is a profound challenge, without getting lost in all there is to 'DO' and 'BE.' Indeed it should be.

Each path is an initiation that prepares us for our future. No initiate gets past the threshold without having gone through the trials it takes to forge a self on the altar of humanity. Some do get lost along the way. Some don't make it to the threshold at all. Some continue to 'wait' to get more and more training and education, waiting for their readiness to do the work.

What if we claimed a readiness? …A sense of already being in the doing of the work right now? What if there was no more waiting? What if when each challenge occurred for us, we recognized it as a signpost that we are headed in the right direction? What if we could turn each experience, each encounter into a necessary tool for our toolbox?

What is needed to make this shift in perception, about who we are and the legend of our lives? How do we move powerfully into our true and overarching identity? How might we be inform and guide our path at an all-new level?

What would be different if we worked from our own understanding of our Archetype and our story? What if we knew our symbols and totems, so that the journey would become a quest instead of just a day-to-day existence? The only distinction between existing and a quest is OUR CHOICE to call our life a quest.

Human beings are made of Images, Form, and Creations. The Image that we hold of ourselves and who we are, informs all of our choices. Our brain, references the past with our memories forming a thought as we make decision. So many of our choices are made from our images of ourselves, combined with our wounds. We must move beyond this response and reaction-based behavior, with a new choice or creation.

Neuroscientifically, employing our right and left brain within our heart consciousness, and using our image of ourselves as our guiding light, we begin to think thoughts we haven't had before.

What if we became our own shero the legend of our own story the maker of our own myth? How would we author our future? How would our personal calling line up collectively with that which is wanted and needed in the world? How would we identify our sacred work in the world?

Who would we need to BECOME and EMBODY, in order to create the future for ourselves, while living inside of who we are now? Who would we INVENT ourselves to be, in order to answer our calling? Transforming our embodiment, in real time, right now?

THE HEROINE'S JOURNEY

The Heroine's Journey is a woman's mythic quest to heal the deep wounding of her feminine nature on a personal, cultural, and spiritual level. She undertakes this spiritual and psychological journey to become whole, integrating all parts of her nature. Sometimes the journey is conscious, but in many cases it is not.

Walking the Goddess Medicine Wheel allows us to lean into the mystery of ourselves the parts of us that we did not even know existed and find our medicine to heal our wounded stories and find our magic. To the right are the 10 steps on the path to wholeness.

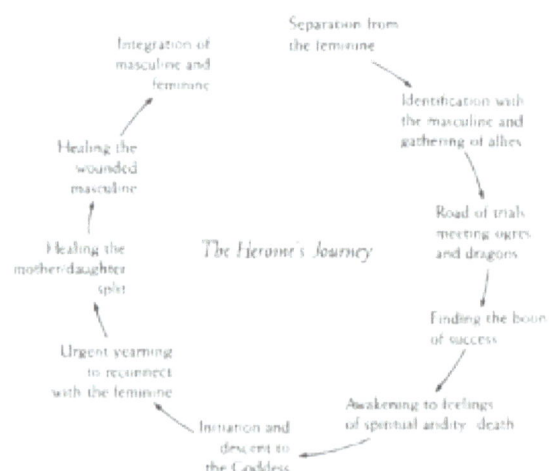

The heroine's journey begins with "Separation from the feminine" and ends with "Integration of masculine and feminine."

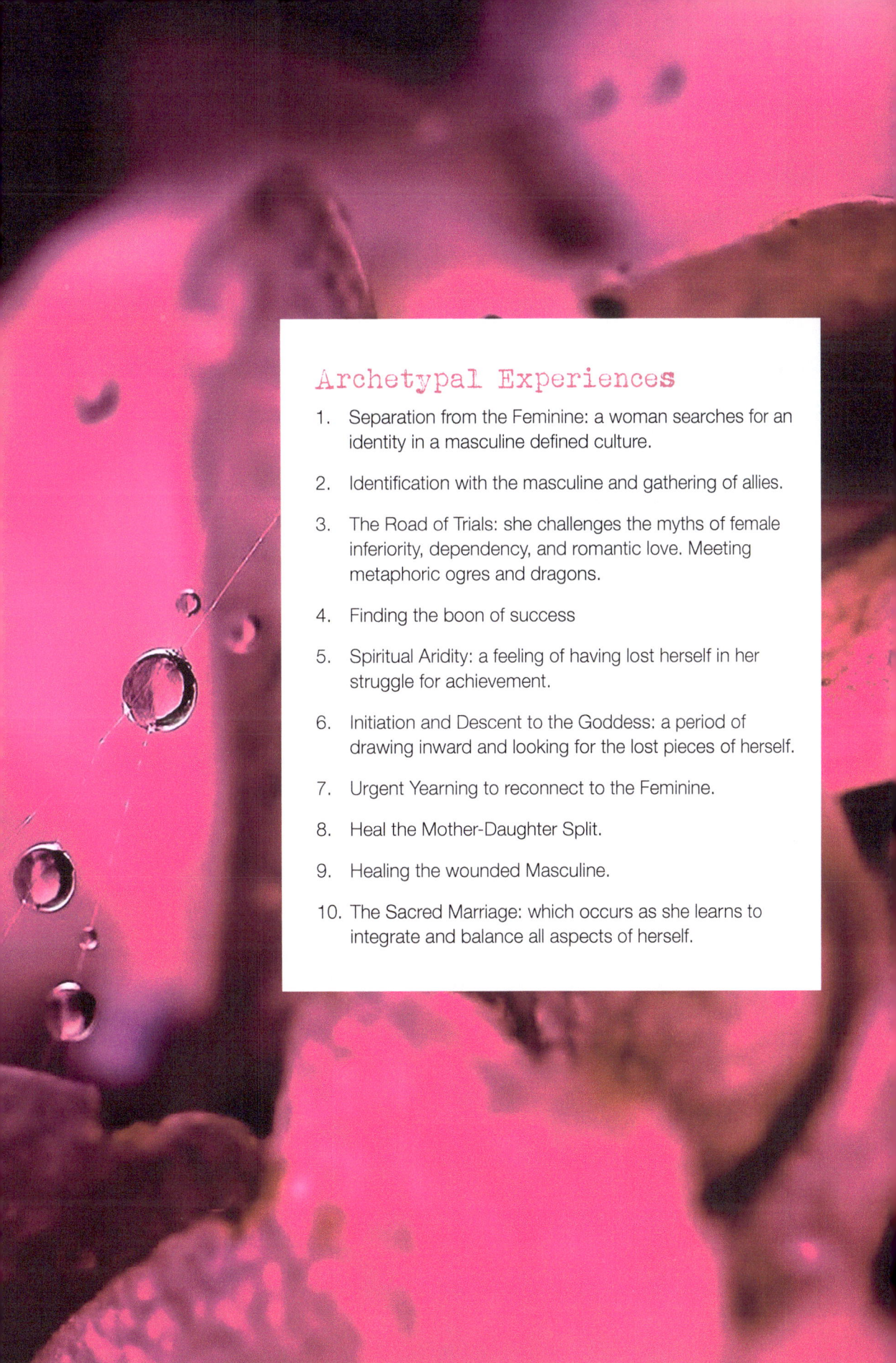

Archetypal Experiences

1. Separation from the Feminine: a woman searches for an identity in a masculine defined culture.

2. Identification with the masculine and gathering of allies.

3. The Road of Trials: she challenges the myths of female inferiority, dependency, and romantic love. Meeting metaphoric ogres and dragons.

4. Finding the boon of success

5. Spiritual Aridity: a feeling of having lost herself in her struggle for achievement.

6. Initiation and Descent to the Goddess: a period of drawing inward and looking for the lost pieces of herself.

7. Urgent Yearning to reconnect to the Feminine.

8. Heal the Mother-Daughter Split.

9. Healing the wounded Masculine.

10. The Sacred Marriage: which occurs as she learns to integrate and balance all aspects of herself.

WALKING THE GODDESS MEDICINE WHEEL

The 5 elements and the 4 directions are archetypal and energetic maps that are as metaphorical as they are very real and embodied. Everything we see, taste, touch, feel, and do can be interpreted through the gateway of the elements within and without. Each element and stop along the wheel can be correlated with a different season, a unique stage of development, a time of day, a physical aspect of our embodiment, and a quality or series of qualities of heart or, as defined here, powers.

Our world, our society, and our culture is heading toward greater and greater complexity. Part of living in a modern, complex world is dealing with a great deal of background noise. The elements are a guide to life and to living life from a connected, simple place rooted in the body, and resourcing from the shared experience of all organic processes in Nature.

The 4 Ways of Embodiment

As we walk the wheel the 4 ways of embodiment help us to round out our understanding of the myriad of ways we as human beings naturally perceive and digest our experiences. Since the Roman Empire and the formation of the Western world, emphasis has been on only ONE of the many intelligences: the cognitive, rational mind. As a leader in your community, and for yourself, it is important to touch in with a more complete and compassionate framework of intelligence - and to check in with all 4 ways of embodiment before performing a ceremony or ritual.

Physical Embodiment: This is the intelligence of the body. It's guides and receptors are our 5 senses: to feel, to taste, to see, to hear, to smell.

It's always a great idea to ground yourself in your body with very simple self-designed stretches or movement meditations that open up the gateway of physical intelligence. This will also help us to activate sensation.

Emotional Embodiment: This is the intelligence of the emotive self. The passing of emotion through the mind, acknowledging any emotions that are present as valid and perfect, welcome for the time being. Its center of activity is the heart.

As you walk with emotional intelligence you are being called into compassion and community. Into a greater knowledge that we are all ONE - the hoop of the people. All emotions, whether they be joy, frustration, sadness, or elation - all are welcome and as wild women, we will never dissipate, quell or stem the flow of this intelligence for ourselves or for others Breathe it in, then let it be.

Imaginal Embodiment: This is the profundity of our imagination. Dreams, intuitions, images, daydreams, patterns, visions, memories and the like, are all powerful gateways into the intelligence of the human system.

We dive into imaginal intelligence through visualization, through description of pattern or maps, through storytelling and our poetic language. We also listen to our 'gut' to 'read' the field and go along with our intuitive senses. We tap into imaginal intelligence when we are given permission to be wildly creative.

Mental Embodiment: This is our old friend. The intelligence of our profoundly capable cognitive minds. Using this level of intelligence we are able to discern, categorize, make clear choices, outline a clear plan and stick to it. This is our organizing mind, so it's also what we call on to help us remember spells, rituals, and right relationship.

Conscious Movement Matters

When brought forth from inside and forged by the desire to create personal change, dance has the profound power to heal the body, psyche and soul." - Anna Halprin

"Movement has the capacity to take us to the home of the soul, the world within for which we have no names. Movement reaches our deepest nature, and dance creatively expresses it. Through dance, we can gain new insights into the mystery of our inner lives.

The field of somatics has developed over the last century through a process of inquiry into how consciousness inhabits the living body. The term is derived from the word "somatic" (Greek "somatikos", soma: "living, aware, bodily person"), which means pertaining to the body, experienced and regulated from within. According to Thomas Hanna, who first coined the phrase, "somatics" is the study of self from the perspective of lived experience, encompassing the dimensions of body, psyche, and spirit.

Somatic movement describes movement that is sensed and shaped from within, rather than from an external source. (ISMETA)

Modes of Perception: The Senses
- Sight - Mirror neurons, the minds eye, and imagination
- Kinesthetic awareness - Feeling which can be enhanced through attention
- Inner senses - Seeing, feeling, hearing, smelling, knowing, and imagination.

SPACE
HOLLOW BONE

What is your soul's deepest longing?

I invoke the powers of space. The deep well of mystery within me. I, call on the guardians of the soul realms to guide me in discovering/deepening/recommitting (to) my (speak your deepest longing). Thank you for walking with me. Blessed be.

SPACE/ HOLLOW BONE

Space Asks: What is your soul's deepest longing?

The elements emerge from space and return to space. It is in this field where all is infinitely possible, all is spacious and quiet. In Tantric Buddhism the Akasha is often described as the 'pregnant zero', the emergent ground of being where impossible emptiness and profound fullness exist side by side. It is here where we all begin, and where we all return: the great cycles of life, death and life.

We can invoke the element of space in our lives when we feel stuck, too small, overwhelmed, directionless, or too empty. Often the space element is associated with our soul - our unique and individual Selves that have journeyed here for a specific purpose – to be and live authentic, wholehearted lives. This soul spark is the source for animating our lives and bodies. It is the depth in our eyes and our prayers for Mystery, for Spirit, for God. To invoke Akasha, is to invoke the poetic and mysterious into the foreground of our lives. To fall back and allow ourselves to be danced.

Powers of Space: Pregnant Potential, and Infinite resource.

Archetypes: The Great Witness, Space-Holder, The Creatrix of the elements, Pregnant Zero, Star Beings.

Imagery: Starburst, dynamic stillness, deep time, the milky way, the void, vacuums, black holes, and crystal clear spheres.

Symbol: Sphere

Type of Energy: Gender neutral. Both projective (masculine) and receptive (feminine).

Form: Pre-thought, and formless

Color: Purple or Black

Direction: All

Invocation: I invoke the powers of space. The deep well of mystery within me. I, call on the guardians of the soul realms to guide me in discovering/ deepening/ recommitting (to) my (speak your deepest longing). Thank you for walking with me. Blessed be.

Physical Embodiment

When you think of having Space in your life what sensations show up in your body?

Emotional Embodiment

When you think of having Space in your life what emotions show up for you?

Imaginal Embodiment

When you imagine having Space in your life what does it look like? What stories comes to mind?

Mental Embodiment

When you think of having Space in your life what actions come to mind?

Notes

IN THE MIDST OF A STORM,
I FOUND THERE WAS WITHIN ME,
A CALM &
A STEADY LITTLE BOAT.

AIR
INSPIRATION

What lays latent in me, ready to be born?

I invoke the powers of air; the guardians of the East, the winds of change, of fresh perspective, of wisdom, insight, and playful purpose. Thank you for walking with me. Blessed be.

AIR / INSPIRATION

Air Asks: What lays latent in me, ready to be born?

Imagine the first light of the sun peaking over the horizon at dawn. Radiant, bright, fresh and new. Associated with our rhythmic in-breath, the Air element ushers forth the possibility for creation, movement, and life. Can you feel how AIR has a way of instigating or beginning a practice? The Air element holds all the qualities of spring, a verdant rushing forth, as gasp for air of a newborn baby, the spark of life. It's time of day is the dawn, just when the golden sun peaks above the horizon to the EAST.

We can invoke the air element when things feel heavy, stagnant, stale and lethargic. You can be sure the Air element will bring you the winds of change, the big picture in all ways both wise, and wily.

The Air element and the direction of the East allow us to take a step back and see with a bird's eye view. Here's a BIG idea: once something is born into the world, creatively and artistically, that movement no longer belongs to you alone. You may have been the conduit, you may be leading the charge, you may be changing lives in your wake, but to hold onto your creation too tightly is to strangle it prematurely while simultaneously closing your creative forces down for the next offering to be born.

The more we know in our body and bones that change is inevitable the more we move easefully and creatively, responding to the needs and whims of the moment in service. What was once the way, may not be the way again. What worked for one student, one day, may not work again. What was once 'yours alone' does not belong only to you again. This is the changeability of life. This is the flow of creation. By attuning to these rhythms we go with the current, riding the tailwinds of the new, instead of struggling against them.

The Air element asks us to be open, vast, and up for anything. Do you feel stuck, uninspired, in a rut, closed-down, too protective, or unclear on what to do or how to lead? The Air element lays dormant, ready to be invoked anew.

Powers of Air: Birds eye view, Holism, Intellect, Speech, Imagination, Inspiration and Creativity, Beginners mind.

Archetypes: Saraswati, and Nimue

Imagery: The creative spark, the east, the aurora, the liminal light that follows pitch black, new beginnings, winds of change, breath of life, trickster energy, wise woman, sacred fool.

Symbol: Feather, and Incense

Type of Energy: Projective (masculine encoded)

Form: Flying, swirling, boundary-less, winged, and wind

Color: Yellow

Cardinal Direction: East

Time of Day: Dawn

Stage of Development: Childhood

Root Race: Asiatic Races

Air Embodied: Respiratory system, and cellular breathing

Invocation: I invoke the powers of air; the guardians of the East, the winds of change, of fresh perspective, of wisdom, insight, and playful purpose. Thank you for walking with me. Blessed be.

Physical Embodiment

When you think of living and inspired life what sensations show up in your body?

Emotional Embodiment

When you think of living an inspired life what emotions show up for you?

Imaginal Embodiment

When you imagine living through inspiration what does it look like? What stories comes to mind?

Mental Embodiment

When you think of living an inspired life what actions come to mind?
What are your beliefs about Inspiration? Who has it? How doesn't?
When do you feel inspired?
What words do you connect with inspiration?
How do they show up in your body? How do they feel when you say them?

Notes

The most important thing is to hold on,
hold out for your creative life,
for your solitude, for your time to be and do,
for your very life; hold on,
for the promise from the wild nature is this:
after winter, spring always comes.

FIRE
PASSION & WILL

What feeds your life force? What no longer serves?

I invoke the powers of fire. The midday sun, the bright flame, the passageway of transformation, the letting go of what doesn't serve. I call on the guardians of the south to see within so that I may act in strong will without. Thank you for walking with me. Blessed be.

FIRE/ PASSION & WILL

Fire Asks: What feeds your life force? What no longer serves?

What I fear and desire most in this world is passion. I fear it because it promises to be spontaneous, out of my control, unnamed, beyond my reasonable self. I desire it because passion has color, like the landscape before me. It is not pale. It is not neutral. It reveals the backside of the heart. - T.T. Williams

Fire has long been sacred to human kind. It has always offered protection, vision, and power to human beings. Internally situate yourself toward the inner south, the place of heat and individual power, the midday sun, blazing overhead erases the shadows in sometimes warming, and sometimes-burning exposure. The fire element feeds on air and for it to be, something must die or shift.

It is because of this that the fire element is associated with transformation, with letting go, and with naked exposure of the true self. Its sense is VISION, which lends itself to self-knowledge, which is ultimately empowering to radically accept who you are meant to be, so you may offer yourself fully to the world. Fire is high passion, reckless abandon, love and radiance, but it MUST be channeled to be beneficial, and not dangerous.

All the unique and individual expressions that begin as an inner impulse, then a vision, then a creation made manifest in the world. It is the Fire element that brought you here, to this training and that fuel your desire to hone your skills. In fact, FIRE runs on desire. This a place to hone yourself, get clear on what you want to offer. Cut through the bullshit that holds you back and keeps you small.

Teaching with fire is about accessing internal belonging with courage - which means to have heart. Doing so will give all your students permission to belong to themselves first too, to birth their expressions freely and affirmatively. To live and breathe their dreams and visions. The South is a place of sacred action and energy. Its powers are those of CHOICE and WILL.

Powers of Fire: Transformation, transmutation, insight, vision.

Archetypes: Aphrodite, Agni, Parvati, and Laksmi

Imagery: Raging furnace, enduring coal, phoenix from the ashes of what is dead, butterfly emerging from the cocoon, midday sun, bonfire, and candle flame.

Symbol: Flame

Type of Energy: Projective (masculine encoded)

Color: Orange

Cardinal Direction: South

Time of Day: Midday

Stage of Development: Adolescence

Root Race: Indigenous peoples of the planet

Fire Embodied: Digestive system

Invocation: I invoke the powers of fire. The midday sun, the bright flame, the passageway of transformation, the letting go of what doesn't serve. I call on the guardians of the south to see within so that I may act in strong will without. Thank you for walking with me. Blessed be.

Physical Embodiment

When you think of living a life filled with passion what sensations show up in your body?

Emotional Embodiment

When you think of living a life filled with passion what emotions show up for you?

Imaginal Embodiment
When you imagine living a life filled with passion what does it look like? What stories comes to mind?

Mental Embodiment
When you think of living a life filled with passion what actions come to mind?
What are your beliefs about passion? Who has it? How doesn't?
When do you feel passion?
What words do you connect with passion?
How does it show up in your body? How do they feel when you say them?

Notes

WATER
INTUITION & INSTINCT

What do you hold for the world?

I invoke the powers of water and call on the guardians of the West. The liminal space before deep sleep. Sundown over the horizon, dusk, twilight. The hunting hour. I call on my own intuitive senses as a deep dream diver, ask for blessings from the whales in the ocean, feel into the resonant song in the waters of the global womb.

WATER/INTUITION & INSTINCT

Water Asks: what do you hold for the world?

We turn to the cooling; healing waters of the West, the place of the setting sun, twilight when the veils are thin and our powers are most potent. We step, one foot in front of the other, into the soothing, resonant, and sensitive embrace of the water element; cleansing, healing, psychic and loving. In it's cool liquidity, it's soft touch, and we are initiated into the receptive, the intuitive, and the inward turning depth of our being.

We are the Holy Grail, the sacred chalice, our bodies; our temples hold both the murky depths of the psyche as well as the surface play of light on clear blue. Water is necessary for our lives and the qualities of water are equally so. We learn to invoke the power of emotional intelligence and uphold its wisdom alongside cognitive activity.

To really be able to SEE the field, we need to remember we are creatures of the deep that thrive on LOVE. Water is LOVE, compassion, understanding and relationship. We hold it all, equally, without judgment. The time of the year is Autumn, both literally and figuratively. It is the time to reap the harvest, the inner bounty, and the accumulation of a life well lived. This is the place where we see our lives mytho-poetically, in images, dreams, visions, feelings, spider webs and stories. Here we live as whales, deep dream divers, dolphins and mermaids.

When we lead with the Water element, we lead from a deep place of love and compassion first. We see the fluidity and connectivity of each particle of water on the planet, connecting us all, nourishing us all, inspiring us all. We lean into our own bodies' emotional intelligence and intuition as a legitimate and essential guiding force. We turn on our empathy and our recognition that we each hold both depth and shallows. It is our job, as a teacher, to create a very safe emotional space for our people, one that is empathic, but not overly heavy.

Powers of Water: Intuition, dream work, compassion, relating, empathy, emotional intelligence.

Archetypes: Quan Yin, Mother Mary, and Poseidon

Astrological Signs: Cancer, Scorpio, and Pisces

Imagery: Rain, teardrops, Deep Ocean, whales, sunsets over water

Symbol: Chalice, cup, well, ocean.

Type of Energy: Receptive (Feminine encoded)

Color: Blue

Cardinal Direction: West

Time of Day: Twilight

Stage of Development: Maturity

Root Race: Caucasian people

Water Embodied: Reproductive system, all bodily fluids

Invocation: I invoke the powers of water and call on the guardians of the West. The liminal space before deep sleep. Sundown over the horizon, dusk, twilight. The hunting hour. I call on my own intuitive senses as a deep dream diver, ask for blessings from the whales in the ocean, feel into the resonant song in the waters of the global womb.

Physical Embodiment

When you think of living a life of intuition & Instinct what sensations show up in your body?

Emotional Embodiment

When you think of living a life of intuition & instinct what emotions show up for you?

Imaginal Embodiment

When you imagine living a life of intuition & instinct what does it look like? What stories comes to mind?

Mental Embodiment

When you think of living a life of intuition & instinct what actions come to mind?
What are your beliefs about intuition? Who has it? How doesn't?
When do you feel the most intuitive?
What words do you connect with intuition?
How do they show up in your body? How do they feel when you say them?

Notes

The most important thing is to hold on,
hold out for your creative life,
for your solitude, for your time to be and do,
for your very life; hold on,
for the promise from the wild nature is this:
after winter, spring always comes.

EARTH
MANIFESTATION

How and from where do you source your power?

> I invoke the powers of earth and call on the guardians of
> the north, my ancestors, those beings of support both seen
> and unseen. I call forth the strength of the unknown, the
> deep silence and the back body, the shadow, to gather round
> in the night, for protection and strength, and to lay to
> rest what is tired and complete. Thank you for walking
> with me. Blessed be.

EARTH/MANIFESTATION

Earth Asks: How and from where do you source your power?

We arrive at the last stage of the wheel, the place of death and quietude of darkness under the midnight sky. New moon energy, the great composting force that is simultaneously the end and the beginning. It is here where we celebrate the sacred landscape of our lives. Our bodies, beautiful at every stage, every wrinkle, every breast that has fed life now sagging, every worn muscle tired now from warrior paths. The earth is associated with our ancestors, the back body, the spine as blade cutting away to build anew. Both our blood lineage and our spiritual, mysterious lineage are standing behind us in great and resourced support. Together we come from the Universe Story.

It is here where we are awed by the majesty of our home, our planet, the Earth Mother; nurturing, moist, dry as sand, dense, stable, unpredictable and wild. In our bodies the earth is our bones and muscles, our support systems, the great sacred geometries of Nature, of form. The earth is burrowing badger and sleeping bear. Tall mountain and deep cave, the power to keep silent, to resource from hidden wisdom in the depths of your soul. This is the time where we reflect and go in to our body temples. In potency, silence and mystery.

When something dies, something is always born.

Powers of Earth: Trust, sacred geometry, boundary setting, letting go, sacred silence, death and rebirth.

God/Goddess Archetypes: Gaia, Diana, Pan, Anna, Innana, Kali, Pele

Imagery: Crone, wise-one, midnight, new moon, caves and dark places, wet earth, towering tree, ancestors, tribal wisdom, the drum, and the rattle.

Symbol: Square

Type of Energy: Receptive (feminine encoded)

Form: Planet Earth; fertile, moist, nurturing, composting, stabilizing soil, inky blackness.

Color: Green

Cardinal Direction: North

Time of Day: Midnight

Stage of Development: Elderly

Earth Embodied: Body structure: bones and muscles

Season: Winter

Invocation: I invoke the powers of earth and call on the guardians of the north, my ancestors, those beings of support both seen and unseen. I call forth the strength of the unknown, the deep silence and the back body, the shadow, to gather round in the night, for protection and strength, and to lay to rest what is tired and complete. Thank you for walking with me. Blessed be.

Physical Embodiment

When you think of manifesting your dream life what sensations show up in your body?

Emotional Embodiment

When you think of manifesting your dream life what emotions show up for you?

Imaginal Embodiment

When you imagine manifesting your dream life what does it look like? What stories comes to mind?

Mental Embodiment

When you think of manifesting your dream life what actions come to mind?

Notes

ALCHEMY

I hope that you will go out
and let stories happen to you,
and that you will work them,
water them with your blood and tears
and your laughter
till they bloom,
till you yourself burst into bloom.

ALCHEMY

Much to his astonishment, C. G. Jung discovered that the ancient art of alchemy was describing, in symbolic language, the journey that all of us must take towards embodying our own intrinsic wholeness, what he called the process of "individuation." As Jung wrote, "I had very soon seen that analytical psychology [the psychology Jung developed] coincided in a most curious way with alchemy.

The experiences of the alchemists, were, in a sense, my experiences, and their world was my world. This was, of course, a momentous discovery. I had stumbled upon the historical counterpart of my psychology of the unconscious." The alchemists, over the course of centuries, had generated a wide range of symbolic images which directly corresponded to the anatomy of the unconscious which Jung had been mapping through his painstaking work with thousands of patients. Jung, in illuminating a psychology of the unconscious, can himself be considered a modern-day alchemist.

Jung continues that "the entire alchemical procedure….could just as well represent the individuation process of a single individual."

The alchemists had little or nothing to contribute to the field of chemistry, least of all the secret of gold-making. Only our overly one-sided, rational and intellectualized age could miss the point so entirely and see in alchemy nothing but an abortive attempt at chemistry.

On the contrary, to the alchemists, chemistry represented a degradation and a "Fall," because it meant the secularization and commercialization of a sacred science. Jung makes the point, "The alchemical operations were real, only this reality was not physical but psychological. Alchemy represents the projection of a drama both cosmic and spiritual in laboratory terms.

The opus magnum ["great work"] had two aims: the rescue of the human soul, and the salvation of the cosmos." The alchemists were dreaming big.ay to rest what is tired and complete.

The ancient art of alchemy was chiefly concerned with changing something of seemingly little value into something precious, of transforming lead into gold, thereby creating the "philosophers' stone" (the "lapis philosophorum"). The "stone," or "lapis," is not a material substance, however, but is an awakened consciousness, which, though seemingly immaterial, pervades, in-forms and gives rise to all creation.

The philosophers' stone doesn't just redeem the individual alchemist, it nonlocally influences the field to such a degree that it was considered to be able to redeem the entire cosmos. The lapis, as Jung emphasizes, is "a psychological symbol expressing something created by man and yet supra-ordinate to him." Alchemy is a timeless, sacred art, as the alchemists' art is to become an instrument for the incarnating deity to make itself real in time and space.

What were you dreams when you were young?

Can you remember WHY you wanted those things?

What are your dreams now?

WHY do you want those things?

So what are your desires?

Think in terms of how you want to feel? How you want to show up in the world. Think about people you admire. What do you admire about them? Your Spirit speaks to you through your desires. They're little whispers that guide us along the way, inviting us. "Follow me, I'm your truth." So lets lean in and get them on paper.

Now let's get your dreams down in writing, answer WHY? Why these dreams? Pick your top 10 and list them below.

Now, answer "What does wild success look and feel like for me?"

Underneath each dream, from your desire list write down the desires that match each dream. (It's O.K. if some of them repeat)

1. _____

2. _____

3. _____

4. _____

5. _____

6. _____

7. _____

8. _____

9. _____

10. _____

Dream 1

Dream 2

Dream 3

How do you move, listen to and nourish your body?

Notes

ALIGNING WITH THE CYCLES OF OUR LIFE

All things are cyclical. The breath, the phases of the moon, the seasons, the stages of development, of life and death, the blood mysteries...all are organic and naturally transitioning processes that provide us with an embodied and connected map to our inner and outer world as we turn with the great wheel of life.

As Wild Woman, it is our task to return to the ways of the earth in remembrance, to bring harmony and balance back to all stages and cycles of the process - where the death and the dying, the aging and the letting go, the doing and the being, are both held in reverence and respect as necessary and sacred swings.

Gaia, the Earth, has sacred structure. She has pattern. In the Tantric tradition, this divine order is called the Krama Shakti. The Power of Order. As women we have lived very close to this order, as its processes cycle through our bodies each month with the letting of our moon blood. As we attune to all the ways the cycle is shown to us, we come into right relationship with both our outer and inner world. We realize we are not separate, but unmistakably interwoven, and the wisdom of the Earth flows through each one of us.

An Animate World

The first step to attuning to Gaia as a living being is in the realization that we live in an animate, alive, and autonomous world, where each living being has their own life's journey, their own karma, their own stories, their own wounds, joys, and gifts. Our egocentric ways - even in the Magic Arts - have placed ourselves as the central character in every interaction with the seen and unseen world.

Often if a hummingbird lands on our shoulder, we'll say, "thank you for coming to teach me, thank you for your medicine!" Living in an animate world is to ask with equal frequency; "what may I do for you?"

To realize each living creature is NOT the central character in your unfolding drama, but that you're in equal and loving relationship is to open yourself up the whole.

Ascendent & Descendent Path

O = Potential. Space. Container. Undifferentiated and Pre-Thought.

Vertical Line = the descent of power. The individual. 1 becomes 2.

Ascendent: Upper World. Unity

Descendent: Underworld. Individual Soul. Fear: What's down here in the dark?

Horizontal Line = Collective: How we relate to others and to our environment. "Middle World".

Elements as Cycles of Creativity

AS CYCLES OF CREATIVITY

Space: Pregnant Potential

Air: Inspiration

Fire: Passion/Will

Water: Integration & Intuition

Earth: Manifestation: Life/Death

Seasons: The Wheel of the Year

Compass: How do we navigate the outer and inner landscape of our lives? How do we feel our way as human beings on the planet? For thousands of years, our orientation has been in relationship to planetary threshold Crossings as marked by the shift of light in relationship to dark.

The ancient peoples knew the importance and the sacred pattern of balance. In some seasons the light is prominent and celebrated, and in others, it is the dark. Every nature-based culture, from the ancient Celtic people to the Aboriginal people in the Southern Hemisphere, celebrated and marked the cyclic wheel of the year.

It's important to remember our root ways, as they continue to affect us today - even though we are often unaware. Like all things, as we bring awareness to the cyclic pattern of light to dark and back again, we simultaneously attune to a harmonic process that can support the unfolding of our own lives.

The following names and descriptions of the seasons are based in the Ancient Avalonian or Celtic tradition.

1. Imbolc
2. Spring Equinox
3. Beltane/May Day
4. Summer Solstice
5. Lamas
6. Fall Equinox
7. Samhain
8. Winter Solstice

High Holy Days:

The Solar Festivals celebrate the height of the season and are determined by the Sun's position in relation to the Earth. Spring Equinox, Summer Solstice, Fall Equinox and Winter Solstice.

Cross Quarter Days:

The Fire Festivals mark the gateway times into each season. They occur half way in between the Solstices and the Equinoxes and are known as the Cross-Quarter Days. Imbolc, Beltane, Lammas, and Samhain.

Imbolc

End of January/Beginning of February in Northern Hemisphere End of July/Beginning of August in Southern hemisphere

The Earth's Awakening

Imbolc is an old Gaelic name term meaning "in the belly." This is the time of year in the northern hemisphere where the first little signs of life are unfolding. The weather softens and the snow begins to melt. Although much of the time is still spent in darkness, this season marks what is being incubated either in the belly, or in the earth. Gestation of the dream is an important practice here, as Nature turns towards creation and the light waxes. Traditionally the Goddess Brigid is celebrated during this time. Brigid is the Midwife who looks over all young life and she sits at the holy well, and tends the sacred flame. During this season, we light candles to Brigid and to the parts of ourselves that nurture new, vulnerable life.

Altar Items: White and blue flowers and crystals, candles, a Brigid's cross, representations of the maiden/youth, pen/paper and vision boards.

Spring Equinox

March 20-23 in Northern Hemisphere

September 20-23 in Southern hemisphere

The First day of spring, Day and Night are Equal

During the Spring Equinox, the holy diad, the masculine and feminine, the light and the dark become balanced. This harmony is the perfect meeting, and creates the perfect conditions for new life to sprout. All of Earth moves into action and expression through the planting of seeds, and the birthing of what has been gestating all winter. Eggs are the symbolic representation of new life, and the ancient way of honoring the Spring Equinox and the resurrection of life existed long before Easter. This is a time of great celebration and right relationship.

Altar Items: Eggs, baskets, feathers, seeds, soft wool or cloth, flowers, amethyst crystals, honey cakes.

Beltane

End of April/Beginning of May in the Northern Hemisphere

End of October/beginning of November in the Southern Hemisphere

Heralding summer, Festival of Fertility

With the waxing of warmth and light, all of Nature begins to dance, and to play, and to express itself. Beltane is the festival of the fire, which represents passion, the creative spark, mischief, and sacred sexuality. With the onset of summer, ancient peoples could finally be outside at night, and so they did - celebrating this cross-quarter day with huge bonfires and love making, lost in the rapture of merging with an other.

The union of the Divine Feminine and Divine Masculine mirrors our outer and inner fertility and enthusiasm for the coming season.

Altar Items: red and orange crystals, phallic/yoni symbols, red candles, red and white ribbons, eggs, rose petals

Summer Solstice

June 20-23 in the Northern Hemisphere

December 20-23 in the Southern hemisphere

Summer's Height, the longest Day and the Shortest Night

Summer Solstice heralds the longest day and the shortest night. Here all things in our world, outer and inner, are illuminated and revealed. We celebrate in a outward, masculine encoded way, with much activity and aplomb, while simultaneously marking what needs to be let go with the coming waning of the light. What no longer serves? Usually at this time of year, it's obvious. Our natural tendency toward action and doing over the summer months very easefully present misalignments and ways we become out of balance. The Summer Solstice is that remembrance that what goes up, must come down.

Altar Items: Seashells, mirrors, summer fruits and flowers, and Tiger's eye crystals,

Lammas

End of July/beginning of August in the Northern Hemisphere

End of January/ Beginning of February in the Southern Hemisphere

Festivals of Gratitude and Marriage

Lammas marks the first harvest festival (Samhain being the last). The grain in the fields is ready to be picked and sorted, and all of the community must gather together to get the work done. Therefore Lammas has been a time of great gatherings and celebrations that delight in the great gift of Nature's abundance. Here we continue our reflection time as we begin to reap the bounty of all that we have sewn that year. Is it a good harvest? What are the manifested results of our work? Our expression? Our dreams?

Altar Items: Ears of corn, wheat, grains, symbolic representations of our accomplishments, hand-made items and crafts, yellow and green crystals and flowers.

Fall Equinox

September 20-23 in the Northern Hemisphere

March 20-23 in the Southern Hemisphere

Festival of Harvest, when Day and Night are Equal

With the waning energy and warmth of the sun, the Fall Equinox is a time to fully appreciate and celebrate the fruits of the season, while preparing for the coming darkness.

Nature is slowing, the fruits are falling from the trees, ready to be picked, canned, and eaten. All of life releases the fullness of Her creation to fuel the next wave of the cycle and to sustain life in the dark months ahead.

The Fall Equinox marks for us a time to let go and to review. All creation, all art, is art for the whole. There is no ownership, no holding on to life at it's peak. Give thanks and let go.

Altar Items: Pomegranates, berries, gourds, pinecones, harvest vegetables, rose quartz and amber crystals, maroon and gold items, art.

Samhain

End of Oct/Beginning of Nov in Northern Hemisphere

End of April/Beginning of May in Southern Hemisphere

The End and the Beginning of the Celtic Year

Gateway to winter season. The very end and the very beginning of the wheel. It's the final harvest festival, where all that is left from the fruit is the dry seed. The essence of something. The greatest potency in the smallest form. Samhain is also a time for slowing down, as the earth does, and reflecting on the season's accomplishments and gifts.

Because Samhain is a powerful time where the veils are thin between the worlds, it is a season of celebrating death as a part of life. Therefore we honor our ancestors, and all who have crossed over.

Altar Items: photographs of loved ones, dark crystals, and seeds of any kind, bones, gourds, pumpkins and apples.

Winter Solstice

December 20-23 in Northern Hemisphere

June 20-23 in Southern Hemisphere

Festival of Rebirth, Midwinter, The shortest day and longest night of the year

The sun is reborn again and we welcome the return of the light. For 3 days and 3 nights the sun appears to stand still and change directions. Winter Solstice marks the longest night and shortest day of the year. All of Nature has slowed down and moved inward, into the belly of the cave. Traditionally, this is the time of year that is the hardest to survive.

Marking the turn from dark to light was celebrated at the midway point of the winter season, and was a hopeful turning point. Christmas, Hanukkah and other season holidays metaphorically mark this birth of the light. It is a time for story telling, celebration, joy and relief.

Altar Items: mistletoe, wreaths (symbolic of the wheel of the year), antlers, anything representative of the sun, cloves, red, green or white crystals.

The Seasons on the Wheel

1. Imbolc
2. Spring Equinox
3. Beltane/May Day
4. Summer Solstice
5. Lamas
6. Fall Equinox
7. Samhain
8. Winter Solstice

Stages of Human Development

1. Death/Birth
2. Infancy/Youth
3. Menarche/Puberty
4. Adolescence
5. Mother/Father Hood
6. Adult
7. Menopause/Middle Age
8. Old-Age

Phases of the Moon

1. New Moon - Emergence
2. Crescent Moon - Rooting/Struggle
3. First Quarter Moon - Action
4. Gibbous Moon - Perfection
5. Full Moon - Illumination
6. Disseminating Moon - Distribution
7. Last Quarter Moon - Re-Orientation
8. Balsamic Moon – Distillation

MOON MYSTERIES AND MENSTRUATION

The moon cycle has 29.5 days, changing from the waxing new moon of increasing light, to the full moon of total illumination, to the dark waning moon of decreasing light, and back to the waxing new moon of increasing light again.

Month after month, the moon cycle mirrors a woman's menstrual cycle, which coincidently has an average length of 29.5 days as well. And similar to the moon cycle, a woman's menstrual cycle changes from the menstruation of new growth, to the ovulation of full power and blossom, to the pre-menstrual phase of harvest and degeneration, and back to menstruation of renewal again. Being able to recognize these cycles allows us to use the most appropriate energy that is available at any given moment. This is in fact a far more efficient use of time and energy.

These phases take on archetypal (or universally recognized) feminine energies as set out below:

- Maiden/Virgin
- Mother/Lover
- Enchantress
- Crone/Wise Woman

Crescent Moon

MAIDEN: Pre-Ovulation

Archetypal Qualities: The word Virgin originally meant a women who was true unto herself. Autonomous, fully fertile, sexual, playful and complete, with no need for any outside affirmation or input. Just like the Virgin Mary, and the buoyancy of youth and springtime, this phase of the moon brings on qualities of independence, curiosity, autonomy, and participation. The forward momentum of the phase invites in fresh ideas and the feeling of being ALIVE within and without.

Waxing moon represents new beginnings and growth. New ideas are being planted. New processes are coming into play. New experiences and events are within reach.

Energy and Activities: The energy of the waxing moon menstruation is inwards and self-nourishing. It's time to think, to learn, to read, and to plan. During this time, you might be open to important learning, to receive knowledge, to set intentions, and to make new plans.

Physical Changes: During this time the body sheds the lining of the old uterus and starts anew. It is a time where we are least fertile. We feel light on our feet, energized, free, and clear. Intellectually oriented and easily stimulated.

Goddess: The goddess associated with the waxing moon is Persephone, a virgin goddess who walked the path to the underworld and was initiated into womanly bleeding. She's the guardian of the crescent moon menstruation.

Full Moon
Mother/LOVER: Ovulation

Archetypal Qualities: Brimming with vigor, passion, energy, love and desire. Outwardly oriented and ready for anything. We are in a state of profound giving and receiving, love, compassion, empathy and trust, centered and at home fully in the heart. Relationships of all kinds are nurtured at this stage.

The full moon represents fire, abundance, power and vitality. It's time to claim one's own power, make decisions, work changes, and bring something into being. To Mother something is to create healthy boundaries, to protect it, to give life force to it and a dedication of energy and intent. This cycle of the month is perfect for making headway on projects that support your growth and evolution.

Physical Changes: The womb is most fertile at this time and the whole body, both inner and outer, radiates with the glow of new life possibility. Estrogen levels are up, making the tissue of the skin soft and the hair glowing. Pheromone levels also spike, encouraging us hormonally to give and receive love and seek beauty.

Energy and Attributes: The energy of full moon menstruation is outward, world nourishing. Feasts and celebration go well with full moon bleeding. The transformational quality of the fire energy makes it an ideal time to learn to transform negative energies into positive ones: rage into creative action, belly cramps into sensuousness.

Goddess: Ishtar, the Red Goddess of Babylon is the guardian of this menstrual fire.

Waning Moon
Enchantress: Pre-Menstruation

Archetypal Qualities: Introspective and Intuitive, we are drawn inwards, to gather our energy for the harvest. Here we reflect on our place and progress in the pursuit of our dreams. We are deeply mysterious, apprenticing to the unseen forces and the magic of the in- between worlds. Here we celebrate the feminine cycle as medicine woman, earth walker, and witch. Internally focused, we can draw others near to us with their perception of the power we hold. We often need to be alone because of this.

The waning moon represents maturity and harvest. It's time for doing by being, for making reality out of the visions and impulses.

Energy and Attributes: The energy of waning moon bleeding straddles the worlds of inward and outward. It is the fruits of our harvest that become world nourishing. It's time to end the blooms of the full moon energy, and to offer them up to Mystery.

Physical Changes: Physical strength begins to decrease. The whole of the body is preparing for menstruation, pulling us into a quieter, less- physically active time. More rest is desired as progesterone peaks.

Goddess: The goddess of this time, Demeter, a mother goddess is responsible for the cycles of life on earth, letting the fruits and grains ripen for harvest, in preparation for the next cycle when she'll withdraw to tend to her own nourishment, letting the earth become barren while she mourns for her daughter.

New Moon
Crone/Wise Woman: Menstruation

Archetypal Qualities: Highly attuned to the dark swing of the wheel, we are in the deep earth mysteries of all that is held in the underworld. We become aware of the full power of the letting go piece, and can wield that power in service of life and right relationship. This wisdom requires courage, introspection and spiritual purpose, and is considered the wisest time for women, where we are in our full power. In ancient traditions, women were often not able to go into ceremony or purification when on their moon blood. This was done not because women weren't honored during this time, but because women's body already KNEW how to purify, and their powers were heightened.

The new moon represents the dark and mysterious power of the deep. Existing structures have fulfilled their purposes, and need to be destructed, or reconstructed to make room for the new.

Energy and Attributes: The energy of new moon bleeding is inwards, self-nourishing. During this time, anxieties, memories, and experiences may rise up, eager to be dealt with. It's a good time to take stock, and to draw conclusions from them. New moon menstruation is a strong time of healing and renewal.

Physical Changes: Release of the uterine lining and unfertilized egg. Water retention and swollen breasts and belly can result in feeling heavy, tired, and slow moving. Rest is needed and a slower pace to the day.

Goddess: The goddess of this time is Hecate, the woman at the joining of three roads, the guardian of mysteries and knowledge, the reaper, the dark one, the crone.

BECOME A FORCE OF NATURE

The House of the Moon is also a great guide to EARTH ALIGNMENT

Why is Earth Alignment important? You'll notice the more aligned you are with yourself, the more your feminine spirit awakens. And the more aligned with your feminine spirit, the more aligned you are with the earth and her cycles and seasons, for nature is the feminine, and your body and the earth are one. You become a FORCE OF NATURE. I'll go deeper below.

The triple goddess and the moon phases

The Triple Goddess refers to the feminine life stages of the Maiden the Mother and the Crone. The phases of the feminine life cycles are also aligned with the moon phases, Waxing, Full, Waning, and, as you'll see below, because EVERYTHING IS CONNECTED, and EVERYTHING IS CIRCULAR, also aligned with the earthly seasons of SPRING/ SUMMER/ FALL (then WINTER- death, and then the cycle starts all over again, because nothing ever truly ends, and every death brings life, every ending a new beginning)

When we are in the MAIDEN (SPRING SEASON/WAXING MOON) stage of life we are like that image of the maiden rushing through the field. Young, rebellious, moving fast and making plans, sewing seeds for our life.

When we are in the MOTHER (SUMMER/FULL MOON) we are at our peak, we are nurturing and giving, bountiful and birthing, at our fullest expression of woman hood and on fire.

When we are in the CRONE (FALL/WINTER/ WANING MOON, DARK OF THE MOON) we are at our wisest, slower, darker, and more mysterious. We receive the most, we do the less, we are one with the mystery of the Divine Feminine. This is portal time, when the veil is thinnest.

In SPRING You feel a reawakening within you a resurgence of energy a newness, a coming back to life of ideas and passion, the self itself, just as the earth thaws and plants sprout and the animals birth babies and the birds begin to sing again. The feminine (yin) and the masculine (yang) are balanced before we tip into more yang. This works in harmony with a WAXING/NEW moon phase, when our energy starts to pick back up, we start taking on new projects, sewing seeds to bloom at the full moon and walking through doors. We are still a bit cautious to not act too fast, but we are moving FORWARD.

In SUMMER You feel on fire with energy, sexually and creatively (which are one in the same, the feminine force of Shakti) as the sun is closest to the earth and we are in our most masculine season, a time of doing, of go go go action, on fire. Yang energy reaches its peak. The seeds we have sewn in spring BLOOM. Summer and the FULL MOON are aligned, things are at their FULLEST. We are in the fullest expression of ourselves, the spotlight is on our lives, we are center stage, so are our projects. Everything is illuminated.

In FALL, When the yin and yang balances again before we tip back into yin, and we start to wane (release, diminish, let go) after peaking. We let what needs to go, go, we are asked to surrender and release what is dying in our lives. The Crone is coming on chilly winds, death for what is dying in our lives is at our doorstep. This time corresponds with the WANING moon, I call it the "LET GO" moon phase. We are in a time of release of that which no longer serves us.

In WINTER we are in the "Crone Zone," we're looking back at our lives, steeped with the wisdom of experience. We're older, wiser, and in that in between tunnel between death and the new life of spring. We're moving in the dark, the only light and warmth is within. We tend to our own inner hearth at this time of year. This time corresponds to the dark of the Moon, in between the waning moon and the new moon. It is time to go slow, listen deeply to intuition, and to not act. To Receive and to be.

KARLI & MARY MAGDALENE

While there are countless important incarnations of the Goddess, the ones I hold dearest, and the ones, in my opinion, most timely in the work of re-awakening the Wild Woman, are KALI and MARY MAGDALENE.

KALI is the Dark Goddess, the ultimate Wild Woman Archetype, the Goddess of the Dark and New Moon, the Great Destroyer of Fear & Illusion. The Greatest lie we could be lead to believe by Patriarchy is that we are separate and alone and therefore our power is limited.

Again and again Goddess Kali destroys that illusion of separation to bring us closer to our truth that we are one with Divinity and one with all that is. If the planet is going to shift, the illusion of separation must be destroyed, and the illusion of fear must be destroyed. Goddess Kali will walk you through the flames of fear into the oneness and endless well of love- the ultimate power- at your center. Again, Sally Kempton's AWAKENING SHAKTI offers wonderful exercises (or exercises) to deepen you into your relationship with Kali.

MARY MAGDALENE is the very heart of the DIVINE FEMININE. She is who you meet at the center of your heart and your very self, she was and is the ultimate Priestess, Prophet, Witch, Whore, Lover, Defender of Truth and Love. She is the ultimate mystery, the ultimate lover, the ultimate mother, she is the very womb of life itself.

INTUITION. The endless work of the feminine is trusting oneself and listening in, RECEIVING the very wisdom - the great power of our intuition - our inner wild woman that sits within us. My favorite go - to practice is seeing our intuition as TRAFFIC LIGHTS related to our CHAKRAS.

At the base, our root chakra, our sense of safety and groundedness our connection to the GREAT MOTHER EARTH, is RED. When we are presented with something and we see RED that is a NO from our internal mother. NOT SAFE, DO NOT PROCEED. This could be DANGEROUS.

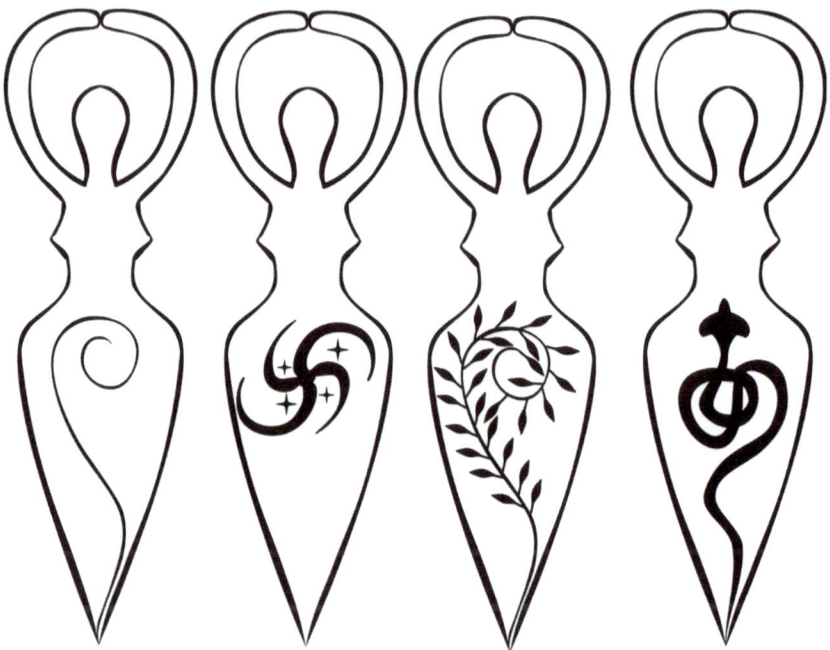

When we are presented with something and we see YELLOW, and feel it in our TUMMY at our sacral center, our sense of self, of whom we ARE, is saying I DONT KNOW/ GO SLOW.

When we are presented with something and our heart, which is the GREEN CHAKRA, OPENS UP, it is saying YES. ALL IN. GREEN LIGHTS LET'S MOOOOOVE. This is great way to talk to your heart. When it OPENS it says YES. When it CLOSES, it says NO.

The last thing I want to offer in this section of the Manual is the importance of PRESENCE. Two books which helped me GREATLY were the FOUR AGREEMENTS by Don Miguel Ruiz and THE PRESENCE PROCESS by Michael Brown. There is nothing that will save you or heal you like the present moment. There is no place safer. NOW is all we have, and now is the only place we have any power.

LAO TZU says it best. "If you are depressed you are living in the past, if you are anxious you are living in the future, if you are at peace you are in the present." Again and again, the present moment will save you.

The work of the Divine Feminine is the work of opening the HEART. The powers of the HEART - LOVE- is the elixir to save the world. The word COURAGE comes from the French word "la coeur," which is heart.

There is nothing braver than to face the world, with total presence, with a wide-open heart. So, we are being escapists when we numb out of the world, by moving into the future or falling back into the past.

We are being Courage-ists when we open our hearts to the here and now. The only time to save ourselves and the planet is RIGHT NOW.

You need you now and the planet needs you now. This is an All Hearts on Deck job, to save this sinking ship. We can do this, together.

Mary Magdalene, in the book, "I REMEMBER UNION," she teaches us to retain our presence. WHEREVER AND WHATEVER may be. First it's about coming into our presence, our divinity, and then it is about keeping it, walking as it.

TRIPLE GODDESS ASTROLOGY

Sun Sign = Heroine. Your conscious self. Your core identity.

The way in which you best are able to express yourself. What makes you feel seen and lit up. Who you are at your core.

Moon Sign = Instinctive Self.

What you know instinctually, or what you need to remember you know instinctually. You emotional needs - what you need to feel emotional secure and able to let go.

Ascendent Sign = How You Dawn on Others. The original imprint of you. Your soul seed. The front line of you in life navigation. How you can best discover who you are as a unique individual.

Aires: FIRE: Cardinal (Initiatory)

Gifts: Initiates, Courage, Individuality

Challenge: Wounded Child, Temper

Taurus: EARTH: Fixed (Stabalizing)

Gifts: Stabilize, Security, Resources, Honor Physical Realm

Challenge: Victim, Scarcity

Gemini: AIR : Mutable (Shifting)

Gifts: Be in dialogue with the world, process data, bridge-build

Challenges: Hermit, airy, overly-analytical

Cancer: WATER: Cardinal (Initiatory)

Gifts: Nurture, be emotionally secure

Challenges: Needly, co-dependent, fearful

Leo: FIRE: Fixed (Stabilizing)

Gifts: Create, embrace self-worth and recognition, play

Challenges : Bully, show-off, vain, no self-worth

Virgo: EARTH: Mutable (Shifting)

Gifts: Be self-contained, be in service, create form, detail

Challenges : Gossip, perfectionist, too wrapped up in the details

Libra: AIR: Cardinal (Initiatory)

Gifts: Balance and harmony, beauty, heathy relationship with all things

Challenges : Slave, too judicious, tit for tat

Scorpio: WATER: Fixed (Stabilizing)

Gifts: Deeply experience life, intimacy, emotional truth

Challenges : Addict, power hungry

Sagittarius: FIRE: Mutable (Shifting)

Gifts: Quest to understand truth, freedom, insight

Challenges : Rebel, wanderer, bliss bunny

Capricorn: EARTH: Cardinal (Initiatory)

Gifts: Self-resourced, responsible, masterful toward a goal, connected to the big why

Challenges: Inner critic, lion tamer, controlling

Aquarius: AIR: Fixed (Stabilizing)

Gifts: True to self, innovative, visionary, community-minded

Challenges : Saboteur, isolationist

Pisces: WATER: Mutable (Shifting)

Gifts: Self-forgiveness, trust in unseen, connect to divine, intuition

Challenges : Escapist, Idealism, loss of imagination

Birth Date:

Birth Place:

Birth Time:

My Sun:

At my core I am :

When I am not in my true self I :

My Moon:

My instinctual self knows she is :

When I do not feel emotionally safe I :

My Ascendent:

I can best discover who I am by:

When I have lost my sense of individuality I:

DREAM TENDING

Dream Tending is the process of orienting your conscious waking self to the dream world as a rich ground of mystery, discovery, hidden clues and secrets, and incomprehensible powers, that rise up at night in the form of images, visitations, emotions, and impressions to help you along your own path of unfolding.

Contrary to what the many dream-interpretation books and sources say, what arises in your dreamscape is unique to you, and it's 'meaning' can only be interpreted by you in the greater context of your life - inner and outer. As Wild Women, we are encouraged to return often to the land of the unknown, unclear, and non-linear, for it is there in the dark where many of our soul powers lie. It is there we can take active part in our own healing and self awareness, and it is in paying attention to the other worlds that attune us to the magic we each hold and wield.

The following process of Dream Tending is inspired and resourced from the book 'Dream Tending' by Stephen Aizenstat. I have personally used this method for some time now to much fruitful and surprising discovery. More than anything, I encourage you to put down the outside interpretations of your dreams, and to withhold the urge to interpret someone else's dream, and let each experience speak to all of us in ways we cannot anticipate.

1. Meet the Dream in the Way of the Dream
2. Open Body Awareness
3. Become Present in the Here and Now
4. Engage the Dream in an Attitude of Not Knowing
5. Ask Core Questions
6. Keep the Dream Alive

"The unconscious sends all sorts of vapors, odd beings, terrors, and deluding images up into the mind - whether in dream, broad daylight, or insanity; for the human kingdom, beneath the floor of the comparatively neat little dwelling that we call our consciousness, goes down into unsuspected Aladdin caves. There not only jewels but also dangerous jinn abide: the convenient or resisted psychological powers that we have not thought or dared to integrate into our lives. And they may remain unsuspected, or, on the other hand, some chance word, the smell of a landscape, the taste of a cup of tea, or the glance of an eye may touch a magic spring, and then dangerous messengers begin to appear in the brain.

These are dangerous because they threaten the fabric of the security into which we have built our family and ourselves. But they are fiendishly fascinating too, for they carry keys that open the whole realm of the desired and feared adventure of the discovery of the self.

Destruction of the world that we have built in which we live, and of ourselves within it; but then a wonderful reconstruction, of the bolder, cleaner, more spacious, and fully human life - that is the lure, the promise, and terror, of these disturbing night visitants from the mythological realm that we carry within." - Joseph Campbell, Hero With a Thousand Faces.

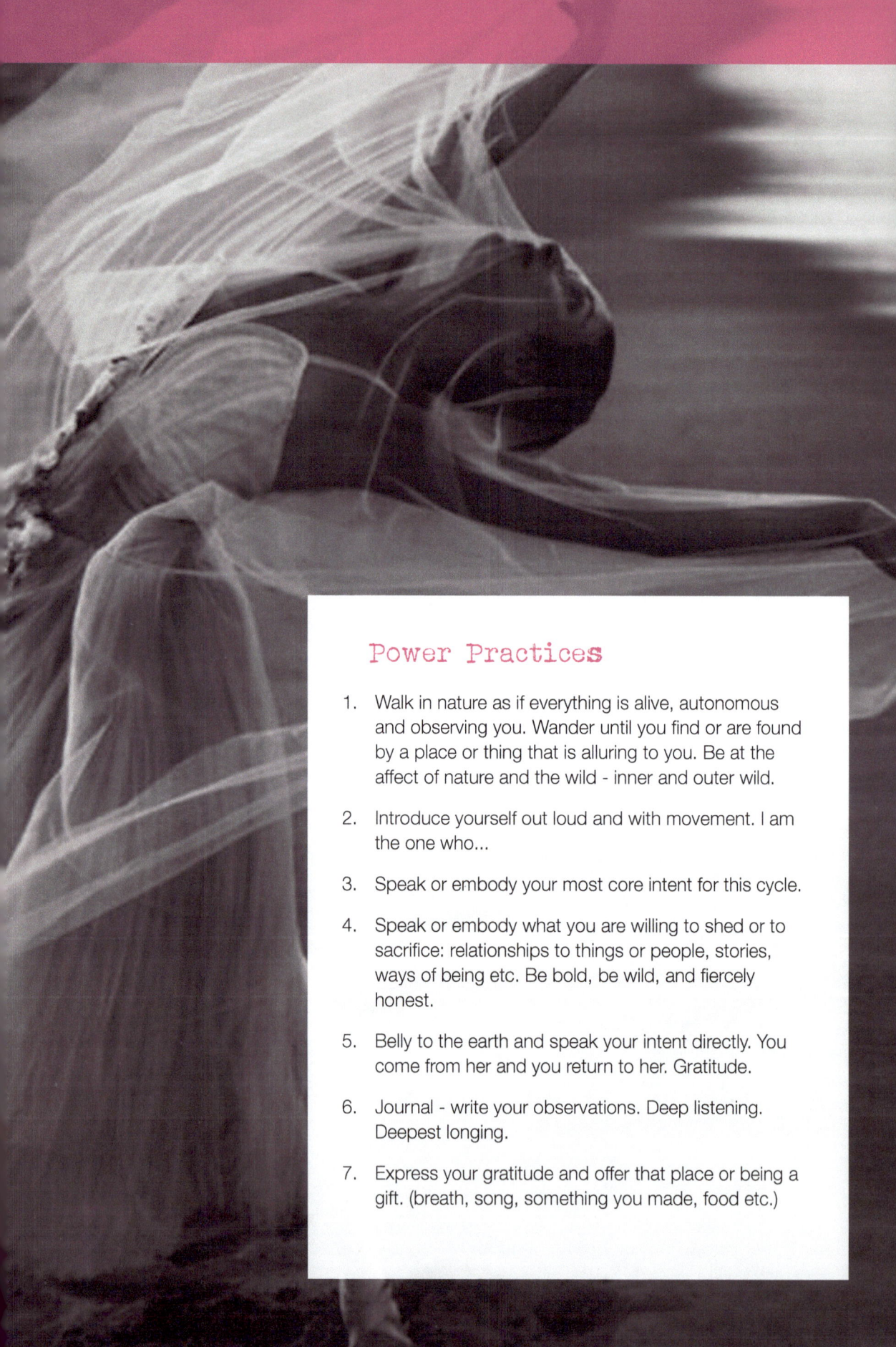

Power Practices

1. Walk in nature as if everything is alive, autonomous and observing you. Wander until you find or are found by a place or thing that is alluring to you. Be at the affect of nature and the wild - inner and outer wild.

2. Introduce yourself out loud and with movement. I am the one who...

3. Speak or embody your most core intent for this cycle.

4. Speak or embody what you are willing to shed or to sacrifice: relationships to things or people, stories, ways of being etc. Be bold, be wild, and fiercely honest.

5. Belly to the earth and speak your intent directly. You come from her and you return to her. Gratitude.

6. Journal - write your observations. Deep listening. Deepest longing.

7. Express your gratitude and offer that place or being a gift. (breath, song, something you made, food etc.)

RESOURCES & REFERENCES

Books:

The Heroin's Journey by Maureen Murdock

Women Who Run With Wolves by Clarissa Pinkola Estes

Hero With a Thousand Faces by Joseph Campbell

Healing with Movement by Anna Halprin

Earth Wisdom by Glennie Kindred

Grandmother Moon by Z. Budapest

Earth Medicine by Jamie Sams

Awakening Shakti by Sally Kempton

The Illuminated Rumi

The Way of Passion: A Celebration of Rumi

Dancing in the Flames: Marion Woodman

Marianne Williamson: A Woman's Worth

The poetry of Mary Oliver

Web Links:

Herbs and Supplies Online:
www.celticherbs.net

ISMETA: International Somatic Movement Education & Therapy: http://www.ismeta.org/

Awakening Avalon:
www.awakeningavalon.com

The Rhythm Way: www.TheRhythmWay.com

On Creating Ceremony:
http://www.llewellyn.com/journal/article/2226

Wisdom of Astrology:
http://www.wisdom-of-astrology.com

Mystic Mama: http://www.mysticmamma.com

Congratulations!
You did it!

Turn your demons into art, your shadow into a friend,

YOUR FEAR INTO FUEL,
YOUR FAILURES INTO TEACHERS,

your weaknesses into reasons to keep fighting.

Dont waste your pain. - *Andréa Balt*

www.ingramcontent.com/pod-product-compliance
Lightning Source LLC
Chambersburg PA
CBHW042009150426
43195CB00002B/66